# GUILT: ITS MEANING AND SIGNIFICANCE

# GUILT
## *Its Meaning and Significance*

BY

JOHN G. McKENZIE

06021

ABINGDON PRESS
New York          Nashville

GUILT: ITS MEANING AND SIGNIFICANCE

*Copyright © 1962 by Abingdon Press*

PRINTED AND BOUND BY THE PAR-
THENON PRESS, AT NASHVILLE, TEN-
NESSEE, UNITED STATES OF AMERICA

# PREFACE

No apology is needed for a volume on Guilt. Our age is riddled with it. It is the theme of our best novels and poetry on both sides of the Atlantic; it preoccupies the minds of the Existentialists; it characterizes not a few of our neurotic disorders; and it is not too much to say that all the great problems of psychiatry are rooted in the debilitating sense of guilt experienced by the psychiatric patient. Ethical philosophers have tended to shirk the problem of guilt, and yet it is essentially an ethical problem; and the concept of guilt raises profound questions both for Law and Theology.

Not a little of the confusion of thought regarding guilt is due to the failure to keep subjective guilt distinct from objective guilt. There has been a strong tendency in psychiatry, especially psychoanalysis, and also in the emotionalist schools of ethics to reduce all guilt to subjective guilt-feelings, and to ignore the fact that guilt-feelings may arise from the violation of some objective standard of conduct whether legal, ethical or religious. The fundamental question of ethics is 'whether moral judgments express desires, strivings, and emotions, or whether they go beyond what is actually desired to what *ought* to be desired'. Does the analysis of guilt-feelings and conscience simply give us a psychological basis for ethics, or does it point to an *ought* and imperative, which as Aristotle said, comes 'from the outside'?

In law there is the problem of assessing guilt or responsibility. Both in America and in England the criteria of responsibility have been the McNaghten Rules. How far do these hold good in these days when psychiatry speaks of 'compulsive tendencies' and impulses that cannot be consciously controlled?

That the new understanding of human behaviour which psychoanalysis and depth psychology have brought us is modifying the legal concept of guilt is shown by the Royal Commission on Homicide's acceptance of Scottish legal concept of 'Diminished responsibility' and by adding emotional disorder to 'defect of reason'.

In ethics we are faced with the refusal of the logical analysts, as represented by Professor Ayer, to allow meaning to moral judgments. Are moral judgments no more than the expression of personal feeling? Is Conscience no more than an emotion? Or are moral judgments judgments of reason?

For religion and theology the concept divides the schools: Is our sense of guilt the mark of our total depravity, or is it the sign that man cannot but seek the loved but lost object, God? Is guilt 'the image of God' seeking its realization, or is it the final proof that the image is totally destroyed?

Both psychiatry and religion are concerned in 'making modern man whole'. There can be no wholeness without the dissipation of guilt. Can psychiatry offer the forgiveness, the faith, the love, the hope, the insight which according to Jung man needs if he is to be whole? Or must religion and psychiatry co-operate? After all, the Church unlike the psychotherapist is not a 'new boy' in the 'cure of souls'. Whatever we may think of theories of the Atonement there can be no question but that the concept of Atonement has brought peace to many a guilt-burdened soul.

I do not suppose theologians are likely to follow my attempt here to base a theory of the Atonement on the psychology of forgiveness. But all theories of the Atonement are out of favour, or shall I say have lost their saving power. And yet forgiveness which alone brings peace seems to demand what the American theologian, Bushnell, called 'cost'. That 'cost' is often paid in morbid self-punishment, as every psychotherapist knows.

These are but a few of the questions which the study of the meaning and significance of guilt raises and with which this volume deals. I have felt that the best approach to the subject was to enter into a thorough psychological study of the origins of guilt-feelings, and the development of the conscience from the birth of the Freudian Super-ego to the rational, positive adult conscience whose guilt-feelings are realistic, and whose moral judgments are rational. Freudian psychology has never been able to give an adequate account of how we pass from emotional and infantile judgments of the Super-ego and the negative guilt-feelings to the mature sense of moral responsibility and shame. Nor do I think that Erich Fromm's 'humanistic conscience' carries us very far. Granted that a true conscience is not 'the internalised voice of an authority we are eager to please and are afraid of displeasing', are we much further on when we are told that conscience 'is our own voice, present in every human being and independent of external rewards and sanctions'? It is said to be the 'expression of our true selves'; but what is the criterion of the true self?

I have not by any means exhausted the subject. I should have loved to have done a chapter on *the sense of guilt in modern literature*, but my references here are limited by lack of knowledge. Critics may think that I ought to have given a chapter to the light thrown upon our problem of guilt by factual studies in the fields of anthropology and sociology. I did consider it; but felt that I could not add to what Dr Rashdall had said in his volume *Is Conscience an Emotion?* when dealing with Westermarck and McDougall. After all, the transition from an emotional sense of guilt to a rational one is not in essence different from the child's passing from the 'borrowed morality' of the Super-ego to a morality rooted in the awakened sense of moral responsibility.

It remains for me to acknowledge how much I have owed to the writers I have quoted, not least to those with whom I have disagreed. As far as I know I have acknowledged all my sources and I trust I have not violated anyone's copyright.

I am greatly indebted to Principal C. S. Duthie, D.D. of the Scottish Congregational College for his careful reading of the typescript and his many suggestions.

To Rev. Professor T. Torrance, D.D., for his notes on Theological Guilt.

To my grandson, John G. Laws, I am grateful for reading the proofs and for helping me with the index.

Finally I pay tribute to the patience of my publishers who have had to bear with several delays before this manuscript was delivered to them. I hope that both they and my readers will feel that the waiting was worth it!

# CONTENTS

PREFACE                                                          vii

1. INTRODUCTORY                                          *page* 13
*Literature and Guilt—Sense of Guilt in Mental
Illness—Law and Guilt—Ethics and Guilt—Theology and Guilt—The Meaning of Guilt—Subjective and Objective Guilt—Unrealistic Guilt—Unconscious Guilt-Feelings—Illustrations—Questions
Raised by the Study.*

2. THE ORIGIN OF GUILT-FEELINGS  *page* 29
*Ambivalence and Anxiety in Children—Growth of
Conscience—Origin of Super-Ego—From the Super-
Ego to the Adult Conscience—Ego-Ideal of Freud
—The Humanistic Conscience—Healthy Sense of
Guilt—Sense of Ought is Ultimate—Awakening of
the Sense of Moral Responsibility—The Mature
Conscience.*

3. THE LEGAL CONCEPT OF GUILT      *page* 58
*Psychiatry in Conflict with the Lawyer—Origin of
the Concept of Diminished Responsibility—Law and
the Psychiatrist—McNaghten Rules—Criticism of
the Rules—Are There Uncontrollable Impulses?—
Unconscious Motive and Crime—American Attitude
to the McNaghten Rules—Oliver Wendell Holmes
and Capital Punishment—Lady Wootton on Mental
Disorders and Criminal Responsibility—Psychological Determinism—Failure to Produce a Concept
of Mental Health—Difficulty of Relating Mental
Illness to Responsibility—The Psychopath—Psychiatrists Have Not Produced a Criterion of Responsibility—The Assessment of Responsibility
Must Remain with the Law—Law and the Moral
Law.*

4. ETHICS AND GUILT                          *page* 87
*Different Theories of the Subject Matter of Ethics
—Protest Against Theological Hedonism—Hume
and Ayer—Linguistic Position of Ayer—Emotive
Theory of Ethics—Teaching Moral Behaviour to
Children—Guilt and Ethical Responsibility—
What Are We Ethically Responsible To?—What*

# CONTENTS

*Are We Responsible For?—Sources of Behaviour—
Motives, Habits, Sentiments, Complexes as 'Systems
of Readiness'—Character and the Self—True Ethical
Guilt Referred to the Self—Freedom of the Self—
Self Possession as Aim of Moral Education—Could
the Self Have Acted Otherwise?*

## 5. RELIGION AND GUILT page 122
*Resume—Religion, Theology and Guilt—Does
Christianity Stimulate Unhealthy Guilt-feelings?
—Illustration of Co-operation Between Medicine
and Religion—Divorce of Guilt from Redemption—
The Theological Meaning of Guilt—Objective and
Subjective Guilt—Experience and Theology—Total
Depravity—Estrangement—Essence and Existence
—The Sense of Ought and Bondage—The Meaning
of Sin—Sin and Ego-Centricity—Sin and Sins—
Object-centricity—Are We Wholly Evil?—Exploita-
tion of God by Parents—Guilt Does Not Demand
Punishment—Guilt is Objective—The Meaning of
Salvation—Guilt as Longing for the Lost Loved
Object—Psychiatrist Has No Technique Whereby
He Could Dissipate Guilt-Feelings of An Objective
Kind—The Psychiatrist's Limitations—The Mean-
ing of 'Wrath of God'.*

## 6. THE DISSIPATION OF GUILT page 154
*Approaches to the Problem of Forgiveness—Psycho-
logical Questions Forgiveness Raises—Psychological
Conditions of Forgiveness—Psychological Conditions of Forgiveness from Man's Side—The Meaning of the Cross—Does God Suffer?—The Triumphs
of the Various Theories of the Atonement—Religious Ideas in Mental Illness—Pastoral Psychology
and Pastoral Theology—Change in the Pattern of
Psychological Symptoms.*

## 7. CONCLUSIONS page 175

### APPENDICES

1. THE URGE TO PUNISH page 182
2. COLLECTIVE GUILT page 187

INDEX page 191

# CHAPTER 1

# INTRODUCTORY

*Literature and Guilt*

IF Professor Hamilton of Winnipeg is anywhere near the truth when he writes: 'Literature is the barometer of the spiritual climate of an age', then our age is not only an 'anxiety-ridden age' as the poet Auden describes it, but guilt-ridden. Even as I write this page Jean Sartre's latest play *Les Sequestrés d'Altona* is running in Paris. Like all his plays it brings out the existential fact that nothing is so personal in man as his sense of isolation and his feeling of guilt. The central figure is Frantz Gerlach eldest son of a wealthy father; for thirteen years after the war he has lived apart from his family in a closed room of the family house seeing only his sister who brings his food but tells him nothing of the outside world. For his part he has no wish to know. In the end, Frantz acknowledges that he is not mourning the lost Germany so much as burdened with a weight of personal guilt. Sartre makes it clear that he is not suffering the sense of collective guilt; but admits and accepts his own guilt; he demands, however, to be acquitted by the future because his age 'was the first to know shame. It knows it is naked.'

Existentialists are not the only writers to stress anxiety and guilt. I need mention only Faulkner of America, Graham Greene in England; Kafka's novel *The Trial* as evidence of this pre-occupation with guilt on the part of authors. The poets are not far behind. Underlying a good deal of T. S. Eliot's poetry there is the sense of estrangement and guilt. 'The world of Sweeney Agonistes', writes Miss Bradbrook, 'is rather like the world of Graham Greene's early novels. The gangsters, toughs, prostitutes and dumb business men are all pursued by hidden fear. The fear is suggested by the ominous pounding rhythms, and heavy repetitions and echoes.'[1]

[1] T. S. Eliot.

## The Sense of Guilt in Mental Illness

Marked as the preoccupation with guilt is in modern literature, the effect of guilt-feelings is seen at its worst in mental illness, and in psychosomatic disease. A central feature in Freud's treatment of morals is his emphasis upon the sense of guilt. He expounds a doctrine analogous to the theological doctrine of *original sin*. In *Totem and Taboo* he contends that morality is a reaction formation against the evil in man. This inherent evil in man he traces to a primitive Oedipus Situation in which the incestuous desires of the band of brothers motivate the murder of the father. The sense of guilt which resulted from the murder is the root both of morality and religion. Morality, he contends, is 'based partly on the necessities of society and partly on the expiation which this sense of guilt demands'. Freud attached great importance to the Oedipus period through which every child passes; any fixation at that period tended to create the sense of guilt which became, when repressed, unconscious guilt. And just as he never departed from his imaginative reconstruction of the primeval murder of the father, so he clung to the idea of the influence of the Oedipal period on mental illness. He believed that the Oedipus period explained the 'ambivalence', that is, the love and hate experienced towards the same person. It is also seen in Freud's belief in the existence of an inherited sense of guilt.

It is irrelevant here to discuss his sociological theories. Enough for the moment to note his findings that the sense of guilt plays a very large part in mental illness.

Dr Stekel, although he diverged from some of Freud's theories, nevertheless laid great stress on the part the sense of guilt plays. In his *Conditions of Anxiety and Their Cure* he went so far as to say that neurosis is the disease of a bad conscience. Like all generalizations, this needs qualification. Yet it cannot be doubted that a great deal of neurotic illness and psychosomatic disease is correlated with guilt-feelings. Often the illness is an attempted escape from the feelings; but not seldom the guilt-feelings are the most prominent symptom.

We tend to pride ourselves on our freedom from Victorian taboos on sexual behaviour; but it would seem that these taboos still exert their condemnation from the unconscious.

## Law and Guilt

Father White in his essay on *Guilt, Theological and Psychological* draws attention to the fact that a good deal of misunderstanding in regard to the meaning of guilt is due to the 'different fields of association which the word "guilt" can conjure up' in different people's minds. 'To the theologian—as well as the moralist and the lawyer—the word will at once suggest something reprehensible and blameworthy; indeed unpardonable except on strict conditions of repentance and amendment. To the psychologist it will suggest more often a pitiable affliction, probably a delusion; a symptom of disorder which causes intense suffering, inhibits life and joy in living and which calls for sympathetic understanding and as little reproach as does physical sickness.'[1]

This misunderstanding is due to a difference in definition. The meaning and significance of guilt is crucial for the lawyer. He is concerned not with the feelings of guilt, but with the objective behaviour which he deems guilty. He is concerned with what constitutes the criminal act. Consciously or unconsciously he is guided by the McNaghten Rules, which I believe influence all our courts of law and not merely the criminal court. They are not merely a definition of what constitutes insanity, but what constitutes a responsible and blameworthy act. If the psychologist defines guilt in purely subjective terms the lawyer tends to define guilt in purely objective terms. He is not concerned with what the individual at the bar feels but with what he did. Nevertheless, as we shall see, the wisdom about human nature which has grown out of depth psychology is not without influence in the courts of law today, e.g. in the concept of 'diminished responsibility'. It is at least a sign that law itself is coming to the position of the psychotherapist and psychoanalyst that there are gradations in the degree of responsibility even in those who

[1] *Christian Essays*, edited by Philip Mairet.

know 'the quality of their act, and know it is wrong'. The problem here is the psychology of the criminal act. Does the psychological analysis of guilt throw light on this?

## Ethics and Guilt

Like Law, *Ethics is involved in the meaning of guilt.* Alas! moral philosophers have shirked the problem of guilt. Professor H. D. Lewis, who is among the few who have made a real attempt to get to grips with the meaning of guilt, introduces his essay on 'Guilt and Freedom' with an implied rebuke of fellow-moral philosophers who apparently refuse to tackle the problem. 'Moral philosophers', he writes, 'do not seem to have had a great deal to say about guilt; and it would be easy to compile an impressive list of ethical treatises in which the subject is not mentioned at all. In recent ethics especially it has suffered much neglect. In theology, on the other hand, the problem of guilt has always been to the fore, and of late it has also elicited the very lively interest of the psychologist. It is the moralist who remains aloof.

'This is as regrettable as it is strange. For however important the problem of guilt may be in some of its bearings, for religious thought or psychology, it is first and foremost an ethical problem. And when the moralists are reluctant to tackle some ethical question, and are content to hand it over to other disciplines, such as theology or psychology, which have an interest in it, the properly ethical features of that question are apt to be either overlaid altogether by extraneous considerations or distorted into some quasi-ethical, religious or psychological form. Of this the treatment of the problem of guilt is an excellent example.'

That Professor Lewis is justified in his regret that moral philosophers shelve the question of guilt no one who knows the implications of a sense of guilt could deny. The study of the concept of guilt and the experience of guilt-feelings must lead to the ultimate questions of ethics. e.g. the nature of moral judgments. Are they no more than the feelings of approbation or disapprobation, or are they the objective judgments of reason? Are the imperatives, whose validity Professor

16

Laird said it was the business of ethics to justify, purely subjective and relative? Would even the morbid sense of guilt with its roots in the fear of consequences have the emotional tone so characteristic of it were it not for its resemblance to real guilt, as Professor Lewis asks?

According to C. H. Waddington man is an 'Ethical Animal', and he means by that that we have an innate tendency to accept moral authority. 'Without an internal system of authority an individual of the species of *homo sapiens* could not become a human person, but the price he pays is to be inflicted, by the excessive development of authority, with feelings which are described as guilt, anxiety and despair. . . .

'Psychoanalysts have discussed extensively the mechanism by which systems having authority are formed within the mind, and the reasons why this process so often, though not inevitably, produces authority which is stronger and more demanding than would seem to be necessary.'[1] In other words there is the problem of the origin of the conscience, whether we think of it in terms of Freud's Super-ego, or the mature conscience, say of a moral philosopher; but not only its origin but its authority. To quote Waddington again: 'We find ourselves coming back from a somewhat unexpected direction to the old apprehension of mankind that eating the fruit of the Tree of Knowledge (functioning as an informing-acceptor) is essentially connected with the knowledge of good and evil, that is becoming an ethicizing being; and also connected with a sense of sin (guilt and anxiety) and finally with a feeling of a need for a super-natural authority.'[2]

Is it not curious that the biologist is compelled to face the problem of guilt while the moral philosophers shirk it? The problem of guilt is, as Professor Lewis contends, a problem of ethics. Leave the problem of guilt, which is the problem of ethics, to the psychoanalyst and we may find the guilt being explained away. As Professor Ginsberg has argued: 'The issue that psycho-analytical theories have to face is that with which all naturalistic ethics are confronted. The problem is whether moral judgments express desires, strivings or emotions, or

---

[1] *The Ethical Animal*, p. 178.    [2] Ibid. p. 178.

whether they go beyond what is actually desired to what *ought* to be desired.' It is the failure to obey this 'ought' which brings guilt. Are there virtues we *ought* to cultivate? Are there duties we *ought* to fulfil? The sense of guilt seems to imply that there are. For there is no guilt unless there is an *ought*, conscious or unconscious, which ought to have been obeyed.

## Theology and Guilt

There is no discipline to which the concept of guilt is more relevant than theology. Indeed it has been said: 'Show that the orthodox conception of sin is impossible and the whole of Christian thinking on the problem of existence is discredited; thus the enemies of Christian Theology. Its apologists likewise count a definite attitude on the subject of sin as a foremost defence against weakening of the Christian position.'[1]

Barth goes so far as to say that instead of speaking about the sin of man, we must speak of the *Man of Sin*. 'Man himself is "in his sins".'[2] 'There is no place for any distinction between himself as the neutral doer of sin, and sin as his evil deed.'[3] To be a sinner is to be guilty. Nothing less than the drama of Incarnation, Atonement and Resurrection can cover man's guilt and make him acceptable to God. Thus practically the whole doctrine of The Person and Work of Christ is related to man's guilt.

The late Dr P. T. Forsyth is no less emphatic as to where the centre of Revelation lies. It is in man's sin and guilt. Contrasting the humanistic attitude to Christ with the orthodox attitude he writes: 'Christ is regarded as central by all who regard Him in a serious way. But central to what? One class of mind sees the whole cosmic issue condensed in human history, all history centred in that of the soul, and the grand symbol of the soul and its meaning set forth for our reverence in Christ. Christ is the spiritual centre of a system of things which is spiritual at last or nothing. He is the grand register of man's confidence in his own spiritual destiny and his power

---

[1] Dr Orchard, *Modern Theories of Sin*, p. 1.
[2] *Church Dogmatics*, p. 407.
[3] Ibid. p. 406.

to realize it, the chief symbol in a long history which can offer the soul no more than symbols of itself. The symbolism of rites becomes in Him the symbolism of personality. He is the great illustration of truths and ideas which must always shine by their own light, and guarantee to an intuition their own power and permanence.

'But another class of mind does not begin with the cosmic problem, even as history, nor with ideas self-luminous and self-sufficient. It begins with the moral problem—of course on a historic scale. It begins with the purpose of God, the Word of God, and man's historic treatment of it. It begins not with the problem of history, but with the revelation in history, not with a problem that revelation may solve, but with a crisis that revelation creates. *Its problem is not adversity but Guilt.* It starts with Christ, not as the Symbol of man's aspiration, or the Hero of his resource but as the Incarnation of God's purpose, or at least as the Prophet of God's will. He is the centre of a system of Grace and Sin. "For the one class Christ is the centre of spiritual Humanity; for the other He is the centre of the will and grace of God." '[1]

I have given enough to show that Guilt is the crucial problem for theology. Its great doctrines of Atonement, Reconcilation, Justification by Faith, and the forgiveness of sin through which both subjective and objective guilt are done away with, can scarcely have meaning without its doctrine of sin and its correlative guilt.

Approaching the problem of guilt from the point of view of man's experience of guilt, can we throw any light upon the nature of man and his relation to God? Is his guilt a sure sign of his total depravity as Barth would say, or a sign of his 'nothingness' as Heidegger would argue? Or is it just a sign of his humanness as Waddington would contend? Is it a sign of his absolute separation from God, or is it the cry of his repressed image of God seeking its source and end? Our sense of sin or guilt shows we are estranged from God; but does not this sense of estrangement and guilt, as Paul Tillich puts it, imply that the estranged being 'belongs essentially to

[1] *Faith, Freedom and the Future*, p. xii f.

that from which one is estranged? Man is not a stranger to his true being, for he belongs to it. He is judged by it, but cannot be completely separated, even if he is hostile to it. Man's hostility to God proves indisputably that he belongs to Him. Where there is the possibility of hate there and there alone is the possibility of love.' Dr Winnicott has defined guilt as 'Anxiety with a special quality'. But anxiety, as we shall see later always involves a longing for the loved object. Does 'estrangement' which is simply another form of guilt imply a seeking for the being from Whom we are estranged?

## The Meaning of Guilt

The late Principal Jacks, long the editor of the *Hibbert Journal,* used to delight in telling the story of two German Professors who were going along a very narrow street where two housewives in opposite dwellings were hotly arguing some point of difference. One Professor said to the other: 'There is little chance of these two agreeing.' 'What makes you think that?' asked the other. 'Well, don't you see they are arguing from different premisses?'

That is exactly what we find, as I have already pointed out, when we come to try to understand the controversy between psychiatry and law, ethics and theology, theology and psycho-analysis in regard to the meaning and significance of 'guilt'. To the psychologist guilt is neither a legal, moral, nor theological dogma, but a lived experience. In other words, to the psychologist guilt is subjective and he defines it in purely subjective terms. He is concerned with the guilt-feelings as experienced by the sufferer. It is quite different with the lawyer, moralist or theologian. Father White has put this difference in a nutshell: 'Although the psychologist will not usually deny that there is such a thing as real culpability, calling for amendment and the sanctions of society, the attitudes towards guilt of the theologian, the moralist and the lawyer will often seem to him quite inhuman and im-mature; while to them, the attitude of the psychologist will often seem unrealistic, amoral, anarchic, perhaps dangerously sentimental. To this a Christian may be inclined to add that the psychologist's attitude betrays a deplorably frivolous attitude to sin and to its terrible consequences in time and eternity; a view which may only confirm the suspicion of some psychologists that religious teachings are compounded of ignorant fears which are a menace to public health and individual happiness. Each party may be so impatient with the other, that it does not occur to either to ask if they are talking about the same thing.'[1]

That is a good description of the confusion which arises when we fail to differentiate between subjective guilt and objective guilt, and between unrealistic guilt and real guilt.

To get a clear understanding of the meaning of 'guilt' let us turn to the dictionaries. Practically all the ordinary dictionaries define the term with reference to responsibility and culpability. It is incurred by some violation of the law of the land; Lewis, the moral philosopher, concluded that 'guilt' is some betrayal of what I take to be my duty by which my conduct becomes directly morally evil and blameworthy'; to the theologian we are all guilty as we are all sinners; we have come short of the glory of God; we are 'estranged', either in virtue of the 'Fall' or because we have outraged the Law of God. To them all we are responsible and culpable. All define guilt in objective terms.

## Subjective and Objective Guilt

So to the dictionaries. One defines it as, 'punishable conduct: the state of having broken a law; crime; wickedness.' 'Originally', this dictionary tells me, 'guilt' was a payment of a fine for an offence, and that it is derived from the Anglo-Saxon word 'gylt' meaning 'to pay'. So the *Concise Oxford Dictionary*: 'The having committed a specified or implied offence; criminality, culpability.'

These definitions imply that guilty conduct is that for which an individual is responsible and worthy of blame. There are two things we have to note here: 1. guilt is attached to the offence; 2. criminality and culpability are legal and moral predicates. They indicate nothing of the guilty person's

[1] *Christian Essays in Psychiatry*, p. 156.

feelings; nothing of his state of mind or his motives. They imply that 'The "guilty" are not merely a menace, they are evil; and the evil nature of their actions is not at all on the level of some functional disorder or disease. It is deep and ultimate.'[1]

When we turn to the dictionary of psychology we find that the term is defined from a purely subjective point of view. Drever defines it: 'Sense of wrong-doing, as an emotional attitude, generally involving emotional conflict, arising out of real or imagined contravention of moral or social standards, in act or thought.'[2]

If we turn to Professor Flügel's thorough and searching examination of psychoanalysis in its relation to ethics we find that the subjective aspect of guilt is far more emphasized than Drever's definition would lead us to expect. He does acknowledge that there are objective moral judgments, and indeed professes to leave their validity to the moral philosopher. One cannot, however, but feel that he thinks our moral judgments are 'orectic', that is, belonging to our emotions or desires, and that if we had fuller knowledge of the psychology of motivation there would be no need for an objective definition of guilt.

What I think we should remember is that guilt-feelings range over a far wider field than either law or ethics cover. Guilt-feelings may be felt when there has been no overt act of wickedness or violation of moral or social standards. In every one of us there is built up, as we shall see in a later chapter, an Ego-Ideal, an image of the kind of person we are expected to be and with which we have identified ourselves. When by thought or act we come short of that ego-ideal we get guilt-feelings. We even get them for tendencies opposed to the ego-ideal of which we may be wholly unconscious. It is these guilt-feelings that come under the notice of the psychotherapist. With these neither the lawyer nor the moral philosopher take much note. Where they both come into close contact is when the psychotherapist avers that guilt-feelings are often the

---

[1] Lewis, *Morals and Revelations*, p. 160.
[2] James Drever, *A Dictionary of Psychology*, p. 111.

cause of crime rather than the result of crime. When we examine the origin of guilt-feelings we shall find that the *Super-ego* or conscience seems to demand not merely obedience or compliance with its dictates, but demands punishment if these dictates are disobeyed. This is the root of what is called 'the need for punishment'. It is the psychological root of the idea that 'guilt must be paid for'; and thus the root of some theories of Atonement as well as of the Sacrament of Penance. Father White goes so far as to say: 'The need to atone for real or supposed guilt is endemic in human nature: the sacrifice of the Cross, which the Church re-presents daily in the celebration of the Eucharist, meets a deep emotional need as well as a rational need without which full atonement is impossible.'[1] In other words *guilt has to be paid for*.

## Unrealistic Guilt

We can see now how it is possible for an individual to suffer from what is called *unrealistic guilt*, and from real guilt with which the lawyer is concerned. Indeed it is not untrue to say that practically all the guilt-feelings which are brought to the psychotherapist interview are related to subjective guilt-feelings and not to overt acts. Guilt-feelings referred to their source may cause regret, shame, remorse but not as a rule neurotic symptoms.

Perhaps the best way to illustrate this fundamental difference between realistic and unrealistic guilt is to take some examples. Let us keep in mind that unrealistic guilt is subjective; objective guilt refers the guilt-feelings to the actual behaviour which has aroused the guilt-feelings. All guilt-feelings are subjective. That goes without saying. The criterion of their reality, their normality, is: *Do they refer to a situation which could account for their intensity?*

Here is the case of a young woman. She was sent because she had developed a 'scissors gait', and was distressed by intense guilt-feelings. She referred these feelings to an incident in her school days in which she had been 'guilty' of curiosity. The teacher had given the class a lesson on the manufacture of chocolate and had illustrated the various processes from

[1] *Christian Essays in Psychiatry*, p. 176.

the cacao seeds to the glossy cake. The patient and another girl were curious as to whether the glossy cake the teacher had shown was real or just an imitation. So they slipped into the class-room during the playtime, and licked the chocolate.

Neither of the girls apparently worried about what they had done. Some years afterwards the patient was to be confirmed. The evening before the actual ceremony the vicar asked the candidates for confirmation whether any of them would like to make their confession before receiving communion on the following day. At once this trifling incident came into the patient's conscious mind. She said nothing, was confirmed the following day. Steadily the intensity of the guilt-feelings increased until she had become a burden to herself and to her parents.

It is obvious that the incident could not account for her misery or the hysterical disturbance of her walk. Guilt-feelings there were but they were displaced and referred to the curiosity and the sampling of the chocolate. In reality she felt guilty not because of this incident but for repressed curiosity about forbidden things. Thus her guilt-feelings were unrealistic. It is to be noted that displaced guilt-feelings always attach themselves to some petty thing which could be construed as reprehensible.

Miss A. came into the room in what appeared a very distressed state. Instead of sitting down she walked round the room saying she had done a horrible thing. When finally she was persuaded to say what she had done to create this state she said that her mother had told her to get a book of stamps from the post office on her way to me. I told her that she could easily get the stamps on her way home. That by no means pacified her. Fortunately I knew her well, and quickly found that she had fallen during the night to a childish habit; instead of attaching her guilt-feelings to this her mind quickly and unconsciously took the first opportunity of creating a scapegoat.

This displacing of guilt-feelings is a species of the wider tendency to displace emotions on situations which have nothing to do with their actual cause. The meek and mild man bullied at work and afraid to retaliate soon picks a fault in his wife or children and thus vents the aggression he was afraid to express in the office or factory. The desires of husbands and wives do not always coincide. Let one of them refuse a request for love-making, and he or she may turn away with the attitude that he or she could not care less. But next day the disappointed husband or wife will find an opportunity to pick a row. Unwilling to accept the fact that he or she was angry at the refusal the anger soon creates an opportunity to express itself without revealing its real cause.[1]

## Unconscious Guilt-Feelings

More baffling to the lawyer, moral philosopher and layman is the psychotherapist's assertion that there is such a thing as unconscious guilt. The guilt-feelings become repressed, but express themselves in various kinds of behaviour.

Not the least noteworthy expression of unconscious guilt-feelings is seen in auditory hallucinations. Here the victim hears voices accusing him of various sins One patient I saw said the voices came from the next house. He would not go out lest he heard the voices or saw the accusers. On one occasion his sister had to bring him to me. Our house was detached from our neighbour's; and at the time the house was empty. Although I told him there was no one in the next house within fifteen minutes he was answering the hallucinated voices.

What happens here is that the guilt-feelings which the conscious refuses to accept and represses come back from the outside world. In other words they are projected upon an imaginary person.

Not so striking but more common is the projection of guilt-feelings and the tendencies which arouse them upon one's wife or husband. The tendencies are not always repressed but they are dissociated from guilt-feelings. Mr B. was a professional man. For about two months he had been violently accusing his wife of infidelity until the situation had become dangerous. Every day for a fortnight I allowed him to tell

[1] Cf. *Man, Morals and Society*, pp. 221 f.

me all the evidence he had of his wife's infidelity. He went back as far as courtship days, and he came up to date on their last holiday! When he brought me his dreams and analysis began of himself, the projection tendency was soon laid bare. For no less than three years he had an adulterous affair with a woman. Three months before I saw him he saw this woman going into a public house with another man. He vowed he would have nothing to do with her again. Within a month he was accusing his wife. The guilty tendencies with their associated guilt-feelings were repressed and projected upon his wife.

What may seem more bewildering to the layman and even to the moral philosopher are the guilty feelings experienced by an individual who is not conscious of having incurred the guilt. In John Atkins's *Arthur Koestler* a whole chapter is given to the sense of guilt which has followed Koestler all his life. 'Koestler', he writes, 'has been hag-ridden by a sense of guilt all his life, over which he has as much control as over a tumour.' Only while enduring punishment did he seem to lose this sense of guilt. 'While he was in prison', writes Mr Atkins, 'in solitary confinement and under sentence of death, Koestler's guilt dropped from him like a worn out cloak. There was indeed no longer any need for it. He was expiating his guilt to the hilt. He was actually being punished for real guilt—for he had gained entry into Franco Spain by deception. His confinements in France and England were much less bearable because they were irrational. He had done nothing wrong. He was merely the victim of wartime hysteria or suspicion. But in Spain reality for once coincided with his psychological condition.'[1]

Even Berdyaev confesses himself a victim of this kind of guilt-feelings. In his autobiography, *Dream and Reality*, he tells us: 'I am inclined to pessimism, although this does not hold full sway over me. I have never been able to believe in the possibility of lasting happiness, which, however, denotes a realism rather than a pessimism. I have sometimes thought that I did not desire happiness: I was apprehensive of it.

[1] *Arthur Koestler*, chapter 10.

Every joy in my life has been accompanied by a sense of guilt and wrong.'[1]

The modern classic on this type of guilt-feelings is Kafka's novel, *The Trial*. K, the hero of the book, is arrested for a crime of which he is utterly ignorant. Nevertheless, he feels guilty and does not know why he should feel guilty. In spite of all his frantic efforts to get help and to know what his crime is he is unsuccessful. He is condemned but never knows the reason why. At the end he is executed.

From what I have written my readers will see why the psychologist emphasizes the subjective side of guilt. To him guilt is neither a criminal, moral, nor a theological dogma but a lived experience. The lawyer sees guilt as something to be expiated by punishment; the moral philosopher is suspicious of psychology lest it claim that moral ideas are derived from an analysis of our nature; moral imperatives are *demands* which, as Aristotle said, come from outside; theology is suspicious of the analysis of religious experience: it can tell us nothing about God or His relation to us. Real guilt, the Barthians would say, can only be understood in the light of Jesus Christ; if we are to understand human experience it can only be as it is seen in the light of the Word of God. No analysis of experience can give meaning to the Word of God or meaning to the doctrine of the Atonement, they tell us.

These positions of Law, Ethics and Theology set us the questions: Can the psychological analysis of the sense of guilt have any relevance to the legal, ethical and theological interpretation of guilt? Might it not lead to a modification of what is meant by responsibility, blameworthiness and culpability? Might it not have a bearing on the vindictiveness of law? We have already spoken of the Need for Punishment; but is there not an urge in us to punish? Would that not influence penalties? Granted that psychology can never be a basis for ethics, yet as Laird has reminded us, behaviour always takes place in a psychological field. 'There is no obligation to pursue a good unless we can see this good and unless the pursuit is

[1] *Dream and Reality*, p. 60.

psychologically possible, at any rate to the best of our belief. Conscience, again is a psychological thing with a moral direction.'[1] Must there not, then, be some relevance in the psychologist's study of the origin and authority of conscience? His study of the growth of moral ideas and their authority? Is there such a thing as authority which is not felt within? To contend that a moral judgment is valid is synonymous with saying it is true. In that case the authority is external. But what is the inward authority of the ought? Only when there is this inward authority do we experience guilt-feelings when the ought is disobeyed. In other words the psychologist deals not with the authority of the moral judgment but with the authority of conscience.

It is important, then, to keep these two meanings of guilt apart; otherwise there can be nothing but confusion. Because it is from the subjective sense of guilt and its resulting symptoms of anxiety-feelings, obsessions, phobias, compulsions and depression that all the great problems of psychiatry have arisen, we must not forget that the problem of objective guilt has given rise to fruitful thinking in the spheres of law, ethics and theology. They must, however, be related. Perhaps we shall see the relationship better when we have studied the origin of guilt-feelings, and the origin and growth of conscience.

SELECTED BOOKS

*Spiritual Problems in Contemporary Literature.* Edited by Stanley Romaine Hopper, New York, Harper's Torch Books.

*The Trial.* Kafka, London, Penguin Books.

*The Collected Fiction of Albert Camus.* London, Hamish Hamilton.

*Man's Search For Himself.* Rollo May, London, George Allen & Unwin.

*Modern Man in Search of a Soul.* C. G. Jung, London, Routledge & Kegan Paul.

*Guilt and Redemption.* Lewis J. Sherrill, John Knox Press.

*Christian Essays in Psychiatry.* Edited by Philip Mairet, London, S.C.M. Press.

[1] *A Study in Moral Theory,* p. 120.

# CHAPTER 2

# THE ORIGIN OF GUILT-FEELINGS

In the introductory chapter I quoted Dr Winnicott to the effect that the sense of guilt is very little more than *anxiety with a special quality*. The words italicized are rather more important than we might think. For anxiety to become the sense of guilt a certain degree of sophistication and self-consciousness must have developed. Guilt, as we have seen, from the psychological point of view, always implies an inner sense of wrong-doing, of self-blame. The vital connection between anxiety and guilt lies in the fact that the sense of guilt originates in anxiety; and anxiety can be experienced by the infant. That is the position reached by recent psychoanalysis; and it is exploited by Dr Waddington to justify his theory that man is an ethical and an ethicizing being.

It seems from these researches that religion, priests and ministers, long supposed to be the culprits in creating the sense of guilt,[1] have been wrongfully accused. As Dr Winnicott puts it: 'The study of the sense of guilt implies for the analyst a study of individual emotional growth. Ordinarily, guilt-feeling is thought of as something that results from religious or moral teaching. Here I shall attempt to study guilt-feeling not as a thing to be inculcated, but as an aspect of the development of the human individual.' That does not mean that religious and moral teaching do not elicit guilt-feelings. Indeed, such teaching may accentuate real guilt-feelings and arouse unrealistic guilt-feelings, as we shall see in a later chapter.

Freud's views on anxiety changed considerably during the years. From a physiological approach he came to see anxiety as a psychological phenomenon and as the antecedent of repression. One idea, however, was common to the earlier

[1] See Guirdham, *Christ and Freud*, chapter 3.

and later views, and that was that anxiety was always 'a reaction to danger', a response to a threat—the threat of losing the loved object. How important that idea is we shall see when we come to deal with the sense of guilt in relation to the meaning of religious guilt-feelings.

Now, if the child-analysts, Melanie Klein, Joan Reviere, Drs Winnicott and Bowlby are anywhere near the truth in their analysis of children, then anxiety-feelings are among the earliest an infant can experience. It is sometimes thought that because an infant cannot formulate ideas its emotional experiences must be very different from that of an adolescent or an adult. That is not altogether true. There are situations which we experience without ideas as Zen Buddhism could show. The experience of the numinous, according to Dr Otto, is completely free of concepts. An infant experiences curiosity long before it can ask: 'What is that?' It can show itself pleased without being able to say what it is pleased with. It can show anger, aggression before it can formulate ideas about the object of its rage. Indeed the most difficult neuroses to cure are those whose roots go back to a period of emotional stress before the infant could formulate ideas.

The infant's anxiety arises from a threat to its dependence, that is the loss of the object on which it depends. It is wholly dependent upon others. That dependence is not felt until there is some kind of deprivation. When that dependence is threatened anger and aggression are aroused. To quote Joan Reviere: 'A baby at the breast is actually completely dependent on someone else, but has no fear of this, at least to begin with because he does not recognize his dependence. In fact a baby does not recognize anyone's existence but his own (his mother's breast is to him merely a part of himself—just a sensation at first), and he expects all his wants to be fulfilled. He (or she) wants the breast for love of it so to speak, for the pleasure of sucking the milk, and also to still the hunger. But what happens if these expectations and wants are not fulfilled? In a certain degree the baby becomes aware of its dependence; he discovers that he cannot supply all his own wants—and he cries and screams. He becomes aggressive. He automatically explodes, as it were, with hate and aggressive craving. If he feels emptiness and loneliness, an automatic reaction sets in, which may soon become uncontrollable and overwhelming, an aggressive rage which brings pain and explosive, burning, suffocating choking bodily sensations; and these in turn cause further feelings of lack, pain and apprehension. The baby cannot distinguish between "me" and "not-me"; his own sensations are his world, *the* world to him; so when he is cold, hungry or lonely, there is no milk, no well-being or pleasure in the world—the valuable things have vanished. And when he is tortured with desire or anger with uncontrollable suffocating screaming, and painful burning evacuations, the whole world is one of suffering; it is scalded, torn and racked too. It is our first experience of something like death, a recognition of the non-existence of something, of an overwhelming loss, both in ourselves and in others, as it seems. And this experience brings an *awareness of love* (in the form of desire) and a *recognition of dependence* (in the form of need) at the same moment as, and inextricably bound up with, feelings and uncontrollable sensation of pain, and *threatened destruction* within and without. The baby's world is out of control, a strike and an earthquake have happened in his world, and this because he loves and desires and such love may bring pain and devastation. Yet he cannot control or eradicate his desire or hate or his efforts to seize and obtain; and the whole crisis destroys his well-being.'[1]

## Ambivalence and Anxiety in Children

The significance of all this for the later experiences of life psychotherapists have seen again and again in their patients. Its fundamental meaning for this study lies in the fact that the need for *security and safety* is awakened at the same time as it is jeopardized. The mother or nurse reacts to this display of anger and aggression in a manner which baby senses as disapproval, and the fear of losing the loved object is also experienced; and that means anxiety.

Take a simple illustration, one easily observed. The baby

[1] *Love, Hate and Reparation*, pp. 8 f.

greedy for the pleasure and the milk finds that the milk is not coming easily or quickly. It gets angry and aggressive and bites the nipple; in return it receives a gentle or an angry slap. Again this is interpreted and rouses the fear of losing the loved object. Thus we have the beginnings of ambivalence— the hate and love towards the same loved object. Naturally this is a growing experience. We do not learn this from observing the infant but from the analysis of older children and adults. All this is occurring in the first twelve months of the child's life. As the child becomes more integrated, he becomes aware of his feelings and behaviour, he is aware of his aggressive feelings and also of his anxiety-feelings. How much anxiety he will experience will depend very largely on the reactions of adults, especially that of the mother. If she is wholly intolerant of these ambivalent tendencies and the child acquires more fear than love, anxiety-feelings are likely to be repressed, and we are likely to get 'tantrums' accompanied by psychosomatic symptoms. If, on the other hand, the mother is patient and always ready to receive gestures of sorrow or regret, then the child will tend to have a healthy anxiety regarding its ambivalent tendencies, and the moral development will be natural. In other words the child accepts responsibility for its feelings however dim that sense of responsibility may be.

The situation of ambivalence becomes more complex with the coming of an infant brother or sister. He (or she) is seen as a rival for the mother's affection and attention. True hate feelings can be experienced towards the newcomer. (Koestler actually struck his brother with a boat hook because he felt usurped.) Naturally these feelings are scowled upon by the mother, and anxiety may now pass into guilt-feelings.

All this, we know, can happen before the child reaches Freud's Oedipus stage when ambivalent feelings of love and rivalry for the parent of opposite sex tend to arise. Freud stemmed the sense of guilt from the Oedipus stage; but now we know the Oedipus complex, if there be one, simply accentuates what is already there. And it is worth noting that the increase of guilt-feelings at this stage is not because of libidinous wishes towards the opposite parent, but because of the death 'wishes', again the outcome of ambivalent tendencies. The boy becomes obsessed with the fear that the father will die or be killed; he may even dream of his father's death. Such fears or dreams, however, are always accompanied by anxiety-feelings, showing conclusively that the child is afraid of losing the loved object. The child does not necessarily hate his father. He wants his mother for himself, yet he loves his father. This desire for the possession of the mother is repressed; the unconscious then throws up ideas how he could possess the mother without guilt. If the father died then she would be his. These death wishes either in phantasy or in dreams are no more than hypotheses; and they should be interpreted as such. The anxiety which accompanies such dreams is not an over-compensation for the death wish, as some psychoanalysts have contended, but anxiety lest the wish come true and the loved one is lost. 'Wish' and 'desire' need to be differentiated. 'Desire' is the idea of an anticipated end, and is conscious; 'wish' is simply impulse energy from the unconscious moving towards an end. The guilt-feelings come from the fact that the 'wish' is the product of the dreamer's own mind; they do not necessarily come from being associated with hate.

I can give a good example from my own experience. When our college moved from the city to the country I was anxious to get a house near the college. There was a very nice house almost at the gates of the college. One very rainy day while rushing the 200 yards to catch the bus back I had the phantasy that the owner of the house had died, and I had sent the Principal's wife to ascertain the price of the house! It was an elaborate phantasy in no more than a few seconds. Personally I did not know the occupier, nor had I any desire for his death. It was a hypothetical phantasy, an imagination thrown up to meet my desire for a house near college.

For anxiety-feelings to pass into true guilt-feelings in virtue of which the child or adult feels culpable there must be some degree of self-consciousness. Just when the child can experience this *anxiety with a special quality*, that is, a sense of

C                                      33

guilt, it is very difficult to say. There can be no question but that it has its origin in the clash of love and aggression.

For a true sense of guilt-feelings we have to wait for the growth of the conscience; it is then that the real moral element is experienced. That undoubtedly begins with self-consciousness. Up to between two or three years of age the child tends to speak of himself in the third person. Challenged by his mother for breaking a cup, he will answer 'John did it'. The day comes when 'John' and 'I' become one. On that day the 'Super-ego' is born, or rather the child becomes aware of it. We may say with Dr Winnicott that this moral organ develops 'naturally in children'; that is to say it comes to birth spontaneously. Dr Waddington, I surmise would say that it is part of our biological equipment. But I doubt it. It is part of the equipment of a potential personality; and its function is to conserve the moral integration of the person.

*Growth of Conscience*

Let us follow its growth and see how it comes to embody moral standards, and why it has such authority.

Looked at from the point of view of a moral process of personality, it is innate; the moral standards, on the other hand, by which we 'ethicize', to use Dr. Waddington's term, that is to judge ourselves and others, are acquired. The child has no innate intuition of what is right and wrong, no innate ideas of the moral quality of emotions, thoughts or behaviour. The approval or disapproval of parents and teachers are his first guides in moral behaviour. In other words, the moral control of the child, at first, is purely external. Its first conflicts are with external frustrations, as we have seen, and with actual external restraints. These conflicts, however, soon become endo-psychic: a conflict between its love and aggression. The aggression is felt towards the external restraint or frustrating object—the breast, and then the mother herself. Moral guilt-feelings are not felt at that stage, only anxiety-feelings. True moral feelings begin, according to Bergson, with a

34

prohibition, with an awareness of the forbidden. Bergson opens his volume on *The Two Sources of Morality and Religion* in the following paragraph:

'The remembrance of forbidden fruit is the earliest thing in the memory of each of us, as it is that of mankind. We should notice this, were not his recollection overlaid by others which we are more inclined to dwell upon. What a childhood we should have had if only we had been left to do as we pleased. We should have flitted from pleasure to pleasure. But all of a sudden an obstacle arose, neither visible nor tangible; a prohibition. Why did we obey: The question hardly occurred to us. We had formed the habit of deferring to our parents and teachers. All the same we knew that it was because they were our parents, because they were our teachers. Therefore in our eyes, their authority came less from themselves than from their status in relation to us. They occupied a certain station; that was the source of command, which had it issued from some other quarter would not have possessed the same weight. In other words, parents and teachers seemed to act by proxy. We did not fully realize this, but behind our parents and our teachers we had an inkling of some enormous or rather some shadowy thing that exerted pressure on us through them. Later we would say it was society.'

We are not concerned at the moment with the source of moral authority; but we may note that Bergson speaks of a 'command', implying that our duties are given us; they are imperatives. The significance of this both for guilt and the sense of guilt we shall see later.

Kurt Lewin, the American field psychologist, says the same thing as Bergson in terms of 'barriers'. The concept of 'barrier' is a general one, and may apply to anything which obstructs us from doing what we want to do. Here we are not concerned with physical barriers; but Lewin speaks of the social barrier which would be synonymous with Bergson's reference to society as the ultimate source of authority of the prohibition or command. Cross this barrier and we have to pay the penalty. But there is also the mental or moral barrier which may carry no penalties; it is the invisible and intangible prohibition. Cross it and we get the guilt-feelings.

How do these prohibitions or moral barriers originate? It is here we find the contribution of Freud and the psychoanalysts. In his concept of the 'Super-ego' Freud opened up the most fruitful field of insight into the sources of guilt-feelings, especially morbid guilt-feelings.

Let me put it in my own words. As we have seen the child's morality begins with the realization of the approvals and disapprovals of parents and teachers. But as Bergson and Lewin note the barriers or prohibitions come from within the child, and pull the child up sharp.

## Origin of Super-Ego

Parents and teachers cannot always be with the child. Hence nature provides the mind with an innate process of introjecting or internalizing the commands and prohibitions of parents and teachers. Take a simple illustration: the child has been prohibited from going to the pantry and helping himself to jam, or of going to the sideboard and helping himself to a Mackintosh's toffee. One day, however, while mother is busy somewhere else he finds himself in the pantry with a jar of jam within reach, or in the dining room with the sideboard door open. He stretches out his hand when lo! the invisible, intangible voice within says: 'You must not do that'; or 'Do that and . . . '. Every prohibition contains a threat. How often have we heard our parents say: 'If you do that again . . . ' and they leave to our imagination what the consequences will be. Commands and prohibitions, musts and must-nots contain implied threats and these threats of imagined consequences are also introjected. They lie over against the personality of the child ready to operate if the command or prohibition is disobeyed.

Let us suppose further that the desire for the jam or toffee is strong enough to repress the prohibition and the child crosses the barrier. Once he is satisfied he is confronted from within with what he has done; the fear of consequences works upon his imagination; and he may conjure up all sorts of punishment; this need not be physical punishment, but the loss of the mother's love, or the sight of his father cross. Memory reminds him that in the past when he had done something 'naughty' and he said he was 'sorry' mother forgave him. There may now be a conflict between the strong tendency to confess and be at one with his mother, and the fear that she will not forgive. There is objective guilt and there are guilt-feelings, both conscious to the child. (Stammer probably commences here.)

Let me put it more strongly still: suppose it is some sexual activity that is forbidden, and the barrier is crossed. Every child senses that the parents' attitude to sexual activity is different from almost any other naughtiness. The emotional tone in which such activity is checked and forbidden is quite different from almost any other prohibition. Here the guilt-feelings and fear of consequences can be very painful indeed, and the child can develop psychosomatic symptoms. The imagined punishments can reach great intensity. Susan Isaacs has listed from her case histories: these 'range in severity from being hard tasks, being scorned, laughed at and reproached, to being put in prison, whipped, deprived of food, starved and done to death in various ways, for instance drowning'.[1]

I had a patient who, invariably in the depressive mood, imagined that he would be put in prison, and indeed could imagine himself there. Total rejection by the loved one is probably the strongest fear a child can have.

These fears are generated by the 'Super-ego'; that is to say, the content of which are the approvals and disapprovals of parents and teachers along with the threats which, as I have said, are left to the disobedient child's imagination.

What we have to note here is that the fear of consequences has become the ideational content of the guilt-feelings; the Super-ego, or as I prefer to call it, 'the infantile or negative conscience' is now demanding the threats to be enacted. (Is this the origin of the concept of Hell?) Unfortunately these subjective guilt-feelings divert the conscious mind, even of the child, from the sense of objective guilt; and the impulses

[1] Quoted by Flügel, *Men, Morals and Society*, p. 53.

which led to the crossing of the barriers are left unmodified. The fear of consequences is the most dangerous type of control a parent or teacher can instil into the mind of a child. Neurotic guilt-feelings in an adult are invariably a sign that the conscience is still in the immature stage of the Super-ego.

There is development in the Super-ego. At a later stage the child does not only internalize the musts and must-nots of the parents, but according to Freud introjects the parents themselves. Dr Karin Stephen puts it this way: 'At this stage these introjected powerful Beings are thought of as directing the child's behaviour from inside according to standards which the child imagines the parents demand from it (which is often a very different thing, in practice, from what they do really expect, because the child's sense of reality is still highly fantastic). Rather later still the Super-ego is thought of as the internal need to conform to an external standard set up by the parents, or parent substitutes, which the child may feel it ought to follow from various motives. It may have to submit against its will, from fear, or it may want to be what they want it to be from love and admiration. In the case of *having* to conform through fear the Super-ego is in conflict with the rest of the child's self and is generally a harsh tyrant against whom it rebels secretly. Its energy is borrowed from the child's own aggressive, destructive revengeful impulses, directed back against itself to deprive it of satisfaction. This "bad" Super-ego is the motive force of the Puritanical Conscience for which all pleasure is sinful.'[1]

Here we begin to find the real roots of unrealistic guilt-feelings. The growing child and the adult do not need actually to rebel; the fact that they have rebellious impulses active in their unconscious mind is enough to give them a horrible sense of guilt. It explains in many cases the guilt-feelings for which the victim can find no conscious explanation.

Recent psychoanalytic research by Melanie Klein, Joan Reviere and Dr Karin Stephen has thrown light upon the ruthlessness of the Super-ego. As we have seen the child

[1] *Science and Ethics* by C. H. Waddington, p. 74.

internalizes the musts and must-nots of parents and teachers, by the process of introjection. When a prohibition or a command is introjected, it is not assimilated; it lies over against the integrated part of the personality without modifying it, like a foreign body. Not only so but it tends to act autonomously, to determine behaviour, thought and emotion without modification by reason or experience. That is why we speak of the Super-ego as infantile. According to these child analysts there is not only this introjection, there is also projection of the child's own aggressive emotions and tendencies. Children seem to be endowed with a great capacity for projection of their feelings on to others. A simple illustration is where a child has done wrong and is ashamed. He projects this shame upon the mother and imagines that the mother is ashamed of him. This tends to increase his guilt-feelings. A far worse situation arises when the child re-introjects after he has projected these hostile feelings upon the parents. To quote Dr Stephen: ' . . . the child projects its own unacceptable impulses on to the outside world and it is these very same projected impulses of its own which it re-introjects and sets up inside itself as its Super-ego. This means that if, for instance, it experiences primitive impulses of rage or cruelty from which it takes flight because its ego is too weak to manage them, it may be obliged to deal with them, instead, by externalizing them, by projection on to its parents and thus it builds up a fantastic picture (called the imago) of these outside people modelled on its own impulses. This picture will be cruel, murderous and also unmanageable and over-powerful like its own repudiated impulses, and when such an Imago is introjected to form the child's own Super-ego this will behave ruthlessly and cruelly to its unfortunate victim, just as savagely in fact as the child wanted to behave when it experienced the impulses, which in its panic, it was driven to project outside itself. The same vital energies which provided the driving force behind the child's own impulses of cruelty, revenge, murder, or whatever it may have been will now reanimate the re-introjected Imago which constitutes its tyrannical and cruel Super-ego.'

Now, many people never outgrow this infantile Super-ego. Unconsciously they strive to obey the prohibitions and conform to the commands. Inwardly they rebel against its rigidity and compulsions; and they may develop what Karen Horney calls a perfectionist character-trend, or a dynamic trend to restrict their lives within narrow limits. The least deviation from perfection and they are full of guilty-feelings, recriminations, and yet at the same time a raging hostility has to be kept repressed, or projected.

Thus we come, again, up against the ambivalence which lies at the root of the origin of guilt-feelings. I would not say that the child or the adult wants to comply with the Super-ego, but he or she fears the guilt-feelings. He or she is afraid of freedom; they are afraid lest the impulses prove too strong for the Ego to control. Hence unconsciously they cling to the authoritative conscience, and yet hate it.

The problem of moral growth is simply the problem of growing up, as Dr Winnicott would contend. We have to pass from Super-ego control to conscience-control. Ideally the Super-ego should 'wither away' like the Communist State. It is doubtful whether the Super-ego ever withers away entirely; but with the development of the adult or positive conscience it performs a different role. Instead of repressing through the guilt-sense an offending line of behaviour, it pulls us up, compels us to reflect upon what we are tempted to do; and then exercises control through reason rather than through feeling. If we cross the 'barrier' and fall then there is a consciousness of objective guilt, but instead of morbid guilt-feelings with all their threats there is sincere contrition, and what the theologians call 'metanoia', that is to say, there is sorrow for the guilty behaviour and a turning away from such behaviour. There is, too, in an adult form a strong tendency to make reparation, a tendency which Melanie Klein found even in young children.

## From the Super-ego to the Adult Conscience

I doubt if we get much help from the orthodox psycho-analysts in this important problem of passing from the negative control of the Super-ego to the free voluntary control of conscience. Dr Karin Stephen thinks we pass from the one stage of moral development to the other when the child obeys, not because it understands the morality of its behaviour, but from love and admiration of the parents and teachers. The energy to obey here is derived not from the fear of the Super-ego but from the child's love impulses. To quote Dr Stephen: 'The particular code of behaviour enjoined varies with the standards set up by the parents (or other admired models) and with the prevailing culture: it may be exacting and may demand renunciations, but the child's wish to obey is whole-hearted and not divided against itself by secret rebellion. It is a love-Super-ego, and it might even be described as "free", voluntary self-regulation following a model which the child has assimilated and made its own, in contrast with the "com-pulsive" submission to an external law which is imposed by the other kind of hate-Super-ego. Willing obedience to a love-Super-ego is sometimes described by Freud as following the Ego-Ideal, and it might be useful to adopt this word and keep the word Super-ego for the punitive kind of conscience which is motivated by fear.'

## Ego-Ideal of Freud

Now, as far as my reading of Freud and Professor Flügel (who has given us the most exhaustive study of the Super-ego) goes I have never felt that their Super-ego theory of conscience can carry us from what is desired to what *ought* to be desired. The sense of objective guilt and the sense of *ought, obligation* and *responsibility* are correlative. Where there is no sense of *ought* there is no sense of objective guilt, and where there is no sense of objective guilt, then, as Dr Winnicott has pointed out, there is a defective conscience. To Freud the tensions felt as the sense of guilt result from the struggle of the Super-ego to hold the impulses in check and the tendency of the ego to allow the impulses to be gratified. This, I believe, accounts for morbid and unrealistic guilt-feelings. Actually it is not a sense of guilt that is experienced but a fear of con-sequences. It is doubtful if there is any realization of the morality of the behaviour. Certainly there is nothing of what can be called contrition, or true moral shame. Morbid guilt is always a moment in the downward thrust of repression, contrition or true shame is the first step in the modification of the offending tendencies. It is a totally different experience from the child's feeling when he has disobeyed a prohibition, or come short of what Freud and Karin Stephen call the Ego-Ideal.

I am aware that Freud repudiated the accusation often brought against him that he ignored the more positive aspects of conscience, and the moral life. In his *Introductory Lectures to Psycho-Analysis* he writes: 'It is no part of our intention to deny the nobility of human nature, nor have we ever done anything to disparage its value. On the contrary, I show you not only the evil wishes which are censored, but also the censorship which suppresses them and makes them unrecognizable. We dwell upon the evil in human beings with the greater emphasis only because others deny it, thereby making the mental life of mankind not indeed better, but incomprehensible. If we give up the one-sided ethical valuation, then, we are surer to find the truer formula of the relation of evil to good in human nature.' [1]

There is not much evidence in that quotation of the 'nobility of human nature'. Surely the nobility of human nature is more than a capacity to suppress evil wishes, or censor them. To make evil wishes unrecognizable would not be the mark of the morally mature man. Indeed it might show that the man was a neurotic. On Freud's own showing every neurotic symptom is in some way an evil wish which has been made 'unrecognizable'.

What I suppose Freud has in mind is his theory of sublimation, an unconscious process by which some purely instinctive tendency which would be socially unacceptable is directed towards a socially useful end. The theory of sublimation depends upon his libido and instinctivist theory of behaviour; and that is questioned today by the neo-Freudians. But along with his theory of sublimation Freud formulated

[1] *Introductory Lectures to Psycho-Analysis*, p. 123.

his concept of the Ego-Ideal. According to Freud this is built up by identification with the father or father substitutes. These become idealized. We may ascribe to them qualities of character which would elicit in us the feeling of their worthiness. We make them worthy of our love. The whole process is subjective and unconscious, and indeed is the fruit of narcissism or self-love. On Freud's libido theory this simply means that some of the libido is directed to ourselves, not, however, as we actually are, but as we should like to be. The realization of the ideal, if I interpret Freud aright, is simply to satisfy our narcissism, or self-love. There is no explanation of objective goodness—or badness of the ideal. The only value of the ideal is to give pleasure by its realization.

All this means that there is nothing in Freud which could account for a real sense of objective guilt. Nothing in Freud's concept of the Super-ego could lead us to the nature of the OUGHT or obligation. As Professor Ginsberg has well put it: 'The central weakness of Freudian moral psychology lies, I think, in its failure to deal adequately with the nature of moral obligation, and this in turn is due to the obscurity which surrounds the treatment of the cognitive and emotional components of conscious obligation; it seems to consist in submission to authority, whether internal or external. The emotional basis is, in either case, fear of punishment or of losing the love of those around us, or of our aggression towards those whom we love. The attitude towards ourselves when the moral sanctions have been internalized retain all the characteristics it had when the authority was external. Nothing is said of the possibility in the advanced levels of moral development or self-imposed rules, or respect for principles of conduct rationally accepted as binding.'[1]

### The Humanistic Conscience

Erich Fromm (as also the late Karen Horney) who still calls himself a psychoanalyst in spite of his deviations from Freudian theory, is perfectly aware of Freud's inadequacy to account for what I should call the mature or adult conscience,

[1] Conway Memorial Lecture.

a conscience which relates the guilt-feelings to objective wrong-doing, the *malum culpae* to the *malum poenae*. He distinguishes between what he calls the 'authoritarian conscience' and the 'humanistic conscience'. The former is characterized by compliance with external authority, speaks much of self-sacrifice, duty and resignation. It is Freud's Super-ego, the internalized authority of the father or father-figures. The 'humanistic conscience', on the other hand, 'is not the internalized voice of an authority we are eager to please, and afraid of displeasing; it is our own voice present in every human being and independent of external sanctions and rewards. . . . Conscience judges our functioning as human beings; it is knowledge within oneself, knowledge of respective success or failure in the art of living. But although conscience is knowledge, it is more than mere knowledge in the realm of abstract thought. It has an affective quality, for it is the reaction of the total personality and not only the reaction of the mind. In fact we need not be aware of what our conscience says in order to be influenced by it.

'Actions, thoughts and feelings which are conclusive to the proper functioning and unfolding of the total personality produce a feeling of inner approval, of rightness, characteristic of the humanistic "good conscience". On the other hand, acts, thoughts and feelings injurious to our total personality produce a feeling of uneasiness and discomfort, characteristic of "a guilty conscience". Conscience is thus a reaction of ourselves to ourselves. It is the voice of our true selves which summons us back to ourselves, to live productively, to develop fully and harmoniously—that is to become what we potentially are. It is the guardian of our integrity . . . humanistic conscience can be justly called the voice of our loving care of ourselves.'[1]

It is very doubtful if this carries us very far in our understanding of the meaning and significance of guilt. Granted that it is a step in advance of Freud's negative conception, we are still left without an explanation of the source of

[1] *Man For Himself*, pp. 158 f.

obligation, a sense of ought to which the sense of guilt is psychologically correlated. That, however, is a problem common to all naturalistic ethics. Apart from that, his *summum bonum* is the old theory of Self-realization, long ago discarded by ethical philosophers. By self-realization he means the realization of all our potentialities. This is not very helpful. Our potentialities are not all desirable by any means. Are we not potentially evil as well as good? His criterion of the good potentialities is 'Productiveness'. How far does this take us? He writes: 'The "productive orientation" of personality refers to a fundamental mental attitude, a mode of relatedness in all realms of human experience. It covers mental, emotional and sensory responses to others, to oneself, and to things. Productiveness is man's ability to use his powers and to realize the potentialities inherent in him. If we say he must use his powers, we imply that he must be free and not dependent on someone who controls his powers. We imply furthermore that he is guided by reason, since he can make use of his powers only if he knows what they are, how to use them, and what to use them for. Productiveness means that he experiences himself as the embodiment of his powers and as the "actor"; that he feels himself one with his powers and at the same time that they are not masked and alienated from him. . . . Productiveness is an attitude which every human being is capable of, unless he is mentally and emotionally crippled.'[1]

To be productive of whatsoever things are pure, honest, lovely and of good report is certainly a mark of the virtuous personality. But the criticism here is not of productiveness, but of what is produced. How can we know the good things to be produced? Fromm's answer is 'listening to ourselves'. Surely this is a dangerous doctrine. Two people listen to themselves and apparently they hear that what they *ought* to produce is quite different and indeed contradictory. To listen to ourselves is to hear only what we desire or unconsciously wish; it cannot give us the objective criterion for which Fromm is searching. He is emphatic on the need 'for objectively valid ethical judgments', believes that the 'humanistic

[1] *Man For Himself*, pp. 84 f.

conscience' can provide them. He believes that the 'true' self can speak authoritatively. But the 'true' self, as Ginsberg has pointed out, is the self as it ought to be, not the self as it is.

One, however, must be grateful to Fromm for the emphasis on the fact that we must outgrow the Super-ego or the 'authoritarian conscience', and the submission to an external authority whether external or introjected is not morality. But I doubt if the 'humanistic conscience' can be equated with the mature, positive conscience.

Later we shall come back to the contribution of psycho-analysis to ethical theory. So far it has not helped us to account for objective guilt-feelings, that is feelings related to some violation of the ethical ought; nor has it helped us to pass from the prohibitive conscience to the mature conscience. Nor can it be said that it has solved the problem of natural-istic ethics, namely, 'whether moral judgments express desires, strivings or emotions, or whether they go beyond what is actually desired to what *ought* to be desired'. It is when the ought is violated that we suffer objective guilt-feelings. Fromm contends that those who are under the domination of an authoritarian conscience or Super-ego have a sense of oughtness. 'I ought to obey my father.' When that ought is violated there is a sense of guilt. But analysis of many persons shows that it is not a case of obeying the father or whatever the internalized authority happens to be, but rather 'I ought not to disobey my father'. It is a wholly negative ought. The victims of an authoritative conscience are not trying to be good; they are struggling *not to be bad*. As Fromm himself has put it: 'Properly speaking, these people do not feel guilty but afraid.' Hence their guilt-feelings are fear-feelings, and thus 'unrealistic or morbid guilt'. They are not striving to realize values, or towards an ideal, but struggling against the fear of crossing barriers of prohibition, commands, musts and must-nots. It is this kind of guilt-feelings which all forms of mental therapy can help.

We are still left with our problem: How do we pass from the negative Super-ego conscience to the positive conscience?

We have seen that Karin Stephen believes that the child passes from the negative conscience when it comes to do things because it loves the mother and wants to please her, and she identifies the positive conscience with the Ego-Ideal of Freud.

## Healthy Sense of Guilt

I believe that the child who comes to obey the parents because he loves them and desires to please them is freer from morbid guilt-feelings and is a happier child. Inter-personal relationships will be healthier; but it would still be a 'borrowed morality'. Here the formula would be, not 'I *must* do as father does', but 'I love doing what he does or says is right'. The Ego-Ideal would still be someone else's ideal although the child has imposed it upon himself. Indeed as Karen Horney has shown, such a motive might easily become a neurotic trend—an indiscriminate need to please others.

We get far more help here from Drs Winnicott and Bowlby. To both the moral consciousness should be a natural development of personality. Dr Winnicott would contend that when the growing boy or girl can accept the fact of their wrongdoing, accept the guilt-feelings which result from their ambivalence or wrong-doing or of crossing the barriers, then the fear of consequences plays a subordinate part. He puts it thus: 'A sense of guilt implies that the ego is coming to terms with the Super-ego. Anxiety has matured into guilt.'[1] That is a healthy development. The child's sense of responsibility for its own behaviour has awakened. This is the beginning of behaviour motivated not merely because the child loves the parents, nor because it fears to lose them, but because in a dim way at first, it *sees* the behaviour was wrong, and experiences the feeling 'I ought not to have done that'. *He not only knows the behaviour is disapproved, but disapproves of it himself. The Super-ego is withering away.*

Naturally, as Dr Winnicott points out, such a state of the growth of conscience is not achieved in one experience,[2] 'this important phase of development is composed of innumerable

[1] *Psycho-Analysis and Contemporary Thought*, p. 19.
[2] Ibid. p. 35.

repetitions spread over a period of time. There is a benign circle of (1) instinctual experience, e.g. (the child taking the toffee); (2) acceptance of responsibility which is called guilt; (3) a working through; and (4) a true restitutive gesture.' On the other hand, it can work in reverse and a malign 'circle' is created; 'there is the undoing of the capacity for a sense of guilt and its replacement by some primitive form of defence'. The result is the fear of consequences, and all the primitive defences against the consequences take the place of the capacity to accept the guilt-feelings and responsibility for the behaviour.

Hence to Dr Winnicott and Dr Bowlby 'A capacity to experience guilt-feelings is a necessary attribute of the healthy person . . . it is part of the price we pay for the privilege of being human (moral) beings'. To put it in my words, the acceptance of guilt-feelings means accepting responsibility for behaviour, and that, as I said, is the first step in passing from Super-ego control to moral or rational control.

Whether these doctors realize all the implications of their position, I am not sure. But it seems to me that they have deviated from the Freudian position. That position is that we are driven by the pleasure-principle and only follow the 'reality principle' to avoid pain in one or other of its forms. To accept guilt-feelings and moral responsibility is to accept moral values, not merely the authority of the father or admired teachers. There must be a degree of moral insight. To Freud and to Professor Flügel moral judgments and moral values are rooted in desire; they are descriptions of a state of mind; their roots are 'orectic' to use a term of Professor Flügel, that is to say they are rooted in the emotional and striving aspects of the mind. When Dr Winnicott and Dr Bowlby speak of accepting guilt as a mark of growing maturity, surely they are speaking not only of what is desired but what *ought* to be desired. It seems to me that there can be no *realistic guilt* where there is no ought to be disobeyed.

Dr Winnicott speaks of this acceptance of guilt-feelings and responsibility as 'coming to terms with the Super-ego'. Actually, as I have contended, it is not a coming to terms with

48

the Super-ego but a leaving it behind; it is the passing from the 'borrowed morality' of the Super-ego to the free morality of conscience where *oughts, commands* and prohibitions have become moral guides and not moral policemen. We accept these not in virtue of external authority, but because we *see* they are true. Indeed to say that moral principles, oughts and commands have authority is just another way of saying that they are *true*. Thus we pass from the negative conscience which functions autonomously and lies over against our personality and indeed is at war with it, to one integrated with our personality. We become inwardly directed by our sense and knowledge of moral values instead of living as though we were 'radar' directed by what other people expect us to be. We respond to objective imperatives, and moral principles because they have what we see as truth.

## Sense of Ought is Ultimate

Now we cannot teach a child, nor an adult for that matter, the sense of obligation or moral responsibility. We can tell a child what his duty is; we can catalogue the virtues; but the sense of *ought* has to be elicited and cannot be directly taught. It may be elicited while we are teaching the duties and virtues; but it may not. Dr Winnicott has a section of his lecture devoted to those in whom 'Sense of guilt is conspicuous by its absence'. 'Undoubtedly', he writes, 'in a proportion of people there is a lack of capacity for guilt-sense. The extreme of this incapacity for concern must be rare. But it is not rare to find individuals who have made a healthy development only in part, and who in part are unable to achieve concern or guilt-feeling, or even remorse. It is tempting here to fall back for an explanation on the constitutional factor, which, of course can never be ignored. However, psychoanalysis offers another explanation. This is that those who lack the moral sense have lacked at the early stages of their development the emotional and physical setting which would have enabled a capacity for guilt-sense to have developed.'[1] On the other hand, the guilt-sense can be

[1] Cf. Hastings Rashdall, *Conscience and Emotion*, p. 28.

49

repressed. I had a patient whose anxiety had for its content that she could not feel any guilt-sense for the life she was living. Actually, had there been no guilt-sense she could not have worried about not experiencing it. Her conscience was repressed; and was not too difficult to recover.

The sense of ought, then, is an ultimate experience. It differs from the moral judgments of *ought*. The judgments are intellectual, and they vary according to culture, and indeed vary a great deal in an individual's life. The sense of ought is a continuant in our experience; the judgment of *ought* is a variant. It is the judgments of ought that differ in different cultures, not the sense of ought.

Psychology has no technique whereby it can guarantee the elicitation of the sense of ought. Like the primary teacher of arithmetic instructing the children how two and two make four; she shows two apples and two apples, two balls and two balls, tries different ways until the children intuitively see the principle. Then it is easy for them to understand the multiplication table. So the psychotherapist interprets this dream, that memory, this experience in childhood or adulthood, this emotion or reaction to frustration until as the Bible puts it, the patient comes to himself.

The sense of guilt cannot be hammered into a child nor for that matter into an adult. He has either lost the sense or never had it. As Dr Winnicott has said, in some it is never elicited at all and in others it is exceedingly weak. To him 'The study of the sense of guilt implies for the analyst a study of individual emotional growth.'

## Awakening of the Sense of Moral Responsibility

In other words, the awakening of the moral consciousness, the sense of moral obligation, of moral responsibility and culpability, is a natural process, in the development of moral personality. It is the dynamic process by which the conscience or moral sentiment is acquired. Like all sentiments it has emotional, ideational and conative aspects, as Shand in his *Foundations of Character* has shown, and like all sentiments has to do with the regulation of behaviour. On the emotional side Shand writes: 'That there is a calm joy in fulfilling the dictates of conscience, and a peculiar sorrow in our failure to fulfil them is familiar to everyone. When we rebel against it, and persist in our evil courses, this sorrow becomes remorse. Its fear is that apprehension of punishment which follows the violation of its laws, and its anger is known as righteous indignation.'[1] Shand thinks that every sentiment has a moral element, and here he is followed by the late Professor Laird and Professor Ginsberg. I believe this is true. There is the professional conscience which curiously enough can be very strong while the general conscience can be weak. On the other hand, when the general conscience is strong and the professional conscience is violated the sense of guilt is intensified. Clergymen and doctors, e.g. are often difficult to analyse because the guilt-feeling stemming from the professional conscience is reinforced by the remorse of the general conscience.

When we speak of educating the conscience we mean the elicitation of the sense of values, the clarifying of moral judgments and principles, the strengthening of the sense of duty or obligation. For that to be effective the innate sense of obligation must already have been awakened. But all aspects of conscience, the emotional, the cognitive and the conative need educating.

In helping the child to pass from authoritarian conscience to the positive adult conscience, that is to say from the stage when morality is regulated by what others approve or disapprove, to that stage when behaviour is regulated by what is believed or seen to be right or what is wrong, the parents or teachers will take every opportunity to show why something is forbidden or permitted. When the child or adult follows a certain course of behaviour because he believes or sees that it is right, reason and the sense of obligation are co-operating. We must not equate intellectual insight with moral insight. One may have well developed intellectual insight without the accompaniment of moral insight. A man

[1] *Foundations of Character*, p. 57.

may be an excellent thinker and yet a rascal; he may be a great artist and yet a great villain.

As I have said, we have no technique by which we could guarantee the awakening of moral insight or the sense of moral obligation. We have techniques whereby we make others comply with our demands. That technique whether used by an authoritarian father, the Inquisition, or the brain-washing agents of totalitarian governments can only elicit the fear of consequences. As the psychoanalysts have shown the home atmosphere is probably the greatest influence; following it I should say the influence of early schooling can be vital. Often the awakening is sudden and devastating. The late Professor Rufus Jones in his *Finding the Trail of Life* tells us that 'The first event of my life which I truly remember is a visit I paid to the house of our nearest neighbour. I wandered off alone hoping no doubt to find there a playmate, a little boy who was a few months younger than myself. On the occasion no one was at home but the door was open and I walked in and surveyed the scene. The little boy's mother, a woman of many gifts, had among her carefully tended plants, a rare and wonderful fuchsia in full bloom. I can see it now with its brightly coloured long hanging flowers. I went up to it with a kind of wild fascination and picked off every one of the flowers. Then I began to feel that all was not well with me. I felt confused and uncomfortable. I couldn't put them on again and so the next best thing to do seemed to hide them. I carried them out and put them one by one down the wide cracks in the steps leading to the porch. I was just finishing when our neighbours drove into the yard. I had the last red blossom in my hand as the mother came up the steps. She went into the house and viewed the havoc and the desolation and returned to tell me what she thought of me as a visitor. Sufficient to say I went home with a very low opinion of myself. What the outraged neighbour said only confirmed what I had already begun to feel inside myself. It is not an accident that this is my first memory. It is precisely the moment when my self-consciousness (moral consciousness) was born. I here suddenly discovered something in myself

I could not altogether control or manage. Something in me reproved me and made me ashamed; something in me hurt me as much as the neighbour's stern words.'[1]

Note that he speaks of 'shame' not fear. Remember also that he was brought up in a Quaker home whose moral atmosphere was preparing the awakening. There was no fear of the consequences; there is the recognition of responsibility and culpability; the experience of shame that hurt. The *malum culpae* and the *malum poenae* are experienced together. That is always the experience of the positive conscience.

The positive conscience is not just a process by which we realise that we have done wrong; it not merely condemns; it not merely prohibits us from doing it again; the experience of self-condemnation changes our whole attitude to the guilty action. We repent in the true sense. There is *poenitentia* (sorrow for what we have done) and there is *metanoia* (a change in mental attitude). To the degree we repent to that degree we can never do the same again. Before this incident the boy probably knew that wanton destruction was disapproved; but there was no sense of obligation to refrain from destructive acts.

In the right atmosphere, then, an atmosphere created by the integrity of the parents and their general attitude to morality (which a child senses) the conscience whose content is no more than the approvals and disapprovals of the parents, passes from the Super-ego into the positive conscience, and there is then a positive orientation to morality. If the parents' affection for the child has elicited the love of the child for them he may spontaneously tend to do what he knows would please them. That may be a step. On the other hand he goes beyond this to the stage when his morality is the outcome not of desire to win their praise but because he desires to be praiseworthy. That is a condition of mind that is conducive to moral insight and the love of virtue. The boy who values honesty has no need to carry a prohibition against stealing; it would never enter his head. So the boy who loves chastity of thought and action is free from the burden of carrying a

[1] *Finding the Trail of Life*, pp. 22 f.

policeman inside of him to block his impulses. The positive conscience refuses spontaneously to be driven by impulse or the offer of immediate pleasure. When the imperious demands of appetite solicit the ego such a conscience gives the power of self-control; whereas the negative conscience may lead to repression and all its miserable sequence. That temptations may be too strong for us is an experience common to us all. The ego may be solicited and fall, *but the Self does not consent*. The ego may be coerced into choosing what the self does not will. The classical experience is that of St Paul, 'That which I would not that I do; and that I would I do not.' As long as the Self does not consent there is no fear of consequences; there is always true shame and contrition.

We never get rid of the negative conscience. It is always there in the background, and even the greatest of the saints have experienced its threats if disobeyed. But its function in a mature conscience is not to threaten but to make us stop and think of what we are about to do; its action often precedes deliberation and choice.

### The Mature Conscience

We are now in a position to define conscience in psychological terms; and from the definition we can see where its authority lies. *Conscience is that sentiment which co-ordinates and regulates our moral ideas, emotions and behaviour according to the moral values, moral ideals, and moral principles we have consciously or unconsciously assimilated. It has an executive function as well as a judicial.* It is a dynamic structure of the Self. If we define Will as the ability of the Self to canalize its energy towards its self-chosen ends, then so far as these ends are consistent with the content of conscience the Will is reinforced by the conscience.

This is a definition of the mature conscience. Its violation leads to realistic guilt-feelings. It is authoritative in the sense that it acts on behalf of the Self as a whole; it is this which gives it authority over every partial impulse. It is related to the fundamental need for moral unity in our lives.

There is the oft quoted saying of Bishop Butler: 'Had

conscience the power as it has the authority it would rule the world.' Psychoanalysis has shown that it has power. It will split a personality rather than allow its moral disintegration. It refuses to condone behaviour contrary to its dictates. Its power can be seen in the process of repression. On the positive side it is the power generated by the conscience that makes an Athanasius stand against the world, a Luther go to Worms, a political leader go into the wilderness rather than identify himself with a policy which his conscience cannot accept; and it fortifies the ordinary man when he is asked to follow a course of action his conscience cannot endorse.

It is not the task of the psychologist to discuss the validity of the authority of moral judgments, or principles. That is the obligation of moral philosophers. The inner authority, the compelling sense of the ought is the psychologist's concern; he is concerned with the guilt-feelings the violation of that ought inevitably brings. He sees the conscience in its initial beginnings as the Super-ego; he watches that passing into the real conscience with the growth of love, intelligence, and social experience. If I may trespass on the biologist's sphere then with Waddington I believe that conscience carries the moral 'genes' of future evolution. Certainly we have our social heritage and that will be enriched; but the vital factor for the evolution Julian Huxley and Waddington anticipate will depend upon genuine acceptance of guilt-feelings, which means a capacity to accept moral responsibility for our individual lives and for the moral progress of the race.

From this survey we are able to see how the psychological definition of guilt as 'Sense of wrong-doing, as an emotional attitude, generally involving emotional conflict, arising out of real or imagined contravention of social standards in act or thought' can be related to the objective definition of lawyers, moralists and theologians. One may be guilty without experiencing any guilt-feelings. This may be due to mental defect or to the defective moral sense of which Dr Winnicott speaks. True realistic guilt-feelings are experienced when the guilt-feelings are referred to the actual wrong-doing; when responsibility is felt; when like Augustine the wrong-doer says 'Mea culpa'; they are referred to an objective situation. Unrealistic guilt-feelings are wholly subjective; they refer to a state of mind, and not to an objective situation. Nevertheless, they may have been generated in the first place by an objective situation; the realistic guilt-feelings displaced then upon a situation which could not account for the intensity of the feelings. On the other hand they may refer to situations which should carry no guilt-feelings whatsoever, because of neurotic character trends, such as morbid perfectionism, or the tendency to restrict one's life within narrow limits.

I had a good illustration from a doctor who had this latter trend. He had occasion to visit a distant friend by car. On the way there he went into a hotel for lunch. He had just an ordinary lunch with no frills or extras, and the bill was quite reasonable. But for the rest of his journey, and indeed when I saw him a day or two after he was still feeling guilt because he *ought* to have thought of the Mission field or of people who could not afford a lunch.

What we have to realize is that feelings of guilt referred to a real objective situation are healthy, 'the price we have to pay for being human beings' as Waddington puts it. The psychiatrist who belittles real guilt-feelings is not doing his duty by his patients. If the guilt-feelings are not dealt with realistically they are likely to be displaced and the mental state of the patient may worsen. Whether the guilt-feelings are unrealistic or realistic they must be brought into full consciousness and dealt with. Only in this way can the victim of a ruthless Super-ego pass from moral infantility to a mature moral adult.

### SELECTED BOOKS

*The Ego and the Id.* Sigmund Freud, London, Hogarth Press.
*Psycho-Analysis and Contemporary Thought.* Edited by John D. Sutherland, London, Hogarth Press.
*The Ethical Animal.* C. H. Waddington, London, George Allen & Unwin.
*Love, Hate, and Reparation.* Melanie Klein and Joan Reviere, London, Hogarth Press.

*Nervous Disorders and Religion.* John G. McKenzie, London, George Allen & Unwin.

*Is Conscience an Emotion?* Hastings Rashdall, Boston, Houghton Mifflin.

*Man, Morals and Society.* J. C. Flügel, London, Duckworth.

*Man For Himself.* Erich Fromm, London, Routledge & Kegan Paul.

# CHAPTER 3

# THE LEGAL CONCEPT OF GUILT

*Psychiatry in Conflict with the Lawyer*

IN turning from the psychological concept of guilt to that of
Law, Ethics and Theology, we are at once confronted with a
problem which more than any other brings the lawyer, the
ethical philosopher and the theologian into conflict with the
psychologist.

The lawyer naturally feels that the psychologist tends to
find an excuse for the criminal act, and has to remind the
psychologist that excuse is not justification. Judges will have
nothing to do with 'Harley-Street-made-law'. The law has to be
administered. As Gregory Zilboorg, the American psychiatrist
has put it: 'The law seems to be afraid that psychiatry might
understand the transgressors too well, and might forgive too
easily. Psychiatry seems to be afraid that the law actively
avoids any true psychological understanding of the trans-
gressor because the law's business is to keep its punitive
promises, and not to wax sentimental by way of scientific
understandings.'[1]

Anyone who has attended a criminal trial in which a
psychiatrist is among the witnesses for the defence will have
sensed the hostility between law and psychology immediately
the prosecuting counsel rises to cross-examine the psychiatrist.
Indeed one might think that the doctor was in the dock, so
severe is the cross-examination. How different is the law's
attitude to the chemist who tells the amount of arsenic found
in the victim's body, or to the finger-print expert, or to the
forensic scientist who identifies a thread found on the prisoner's clothes with the material the victim was wearing at the
time of the crime! No type of witness can be made to look
so much like a fool as a defending psychiatrist. It is much

[1] *Psychology of the Criminal Act*, p. 13.

easier to witness to the sanity of the prisoner than to explain to a judge or jury the effect of an unconscious but compelling motive, or character-tendencies of a neurotic kind, which throw light upon the state of mind of the accused. From the judge and jury's observation of the prisoner he may look intelligent, well balanced and rational. No staring eyes, no drooling at the mouth. On the contrary, he seems to be taking an intelligent interest in the proceedings. Psychoanalytic jargon is a foreign language to the jury and bores rather than impresses them.

## Origin of the Concept of Diminished Responsibility

On the other hand, one cannot read through Granville Williams's Hamlyn Lectures on *The Proof of Guilt* without realizing the care that is taken by the law to see that no innocent man will be unjustly punished.

One of the interesting legal stories is the origin of the concept of 'Diminished Responsibility' as told by Lord Keith in an address on 'Some Observations on Diminished Responsibility'. 'It is interesting', said the learned judge, 'to look at the first recognizable case of the application of the doctrine of "diminished responsibility" in a case charged as murder. The case is Her Majesty's Advocate *v.* Dingwall, tried in 1867. The accused had stabbed his wife with a carving knife in the early hours of January 1st, 1867. He was addicted to drink and during the day of December 31st, mostly between 4 p.m. and midnight, he had drunk eleven glasses of whisky. The cause of the attack may have been annoyance at his wife for concealing a bottle of whisky which he had brought home with him. Various points were dealt with by the trial judge in his charge to the jury, including intoxication and insanity. He charged against the prisoner on the intoxication issue, and left the insanity issue to the jury. He then directed the jury to the question whether the offence was something short of murder. Among the considerations referred to were that the prisoner appeared to be not only peculiar in his mental constitution but to have had his mind weakened by successive attacks of disease. It seemed probable he had sunstroke in

India and fits of an epileptic nature. He had had repeated attacks of delirium tremens. The direction to the jury, as given in the report, was as follows: "The state of mind of a prisoner might be an extenuating circumstance, although not such as to warrant an acquittal on the ground of insanity, and he could not therefore exclude it from the consideration of the jury here, along with the whole other circumstances, in making up their minds whether, if responsible to the law at all, the prisoner was to be held guilty of murder or culpable homicide." The jury returned a verdict of culpable homicide and the prisoner was sentenced to ten years' penal servitude.'

As an interesting note to this is the fact that Lord Deas who tried the case continued to 'direct juries to similar affect in a number of cases down to the date of his retirement'. And another case cited by Lord Keith shows that his concept influenced his fellow-judges until it became a recognized feature of Scottish judicial procedure. It was not, however, until 1909 that the phrase 'diminished responsibility' came into general use. Now it has become incorporated in the Homicidal Act of England.

Of Lord Deas the *Scotsman* in its obituary notice wrote: 'He was indeed—and we state the chief if not the only blot in his judicial character when we say so—too eager for conviction and in questions of guilt or innocence a little too ready to assume his own omniscience and that of doctors and detectives not half so scrupulous as himself. Still be it also set down to his credit that he often manifested a singular kindly consideration for respectable men and good-looking women who did not belong to the criminal classes and who had landed in the dock by one sudden explosion of passion or by one false step.'

I have given this story in detail to show that even before psychiatry in the person of Isaac Ray of America protested against the McNaghten Rules, or Maudsley of England, law went out of its way to see that responsibility for criminal acts was rightly assessed.

That does not mean that law accepted the expert evidence of the psychiatrist as readily as it accepts the evidence of the

forensic scientist. Far from it. After all, the evidence of the
forensic experts is objective and is there for anyone to see;
the amount of arsenic in a body can be measured as well as
demonstrated. The evidence of the psychiatrist is based on
his appraisement of the subjective condition of the accused's
mind. And he is not a little influenced, perhaps more than he
realizes, by his own emotional attitude and his psychological
theories.

Apart from that psychology can hardly be said to be a body
of fundamental principles or concepts universally accepted
by psychologists themselves. It is not a case of difference in
the application of accepted concepts that is common to all
science. The differences between psychologists themselves
reach down to the motivation of behaviour. Here is a description of psychology by Professor Cohen, the Psychology
Professor of Manchester University: 'Psychology is the most
undisciplined of disciplines, the nursery and romping ground
for every extravaganza, a Tower of Babel for every known
and unknown tongue, a mint for counterfeit and spurious
coins, a market-place for every pedlar of far-fetched and
unlikely theories. It is an amalgam of humbug, platitude,
piercing intuition, naïvete, soaring flight of imagination, dull
dogma, incisive reasoning and sheer drivel. . . . Every text-
book on the shelves of the psychological library should have
inscribed on it the number of grains of salt to be taken when
reading it, and on the library table an ample bowl of salt
should be placed and replenished at regular intervals. Certain
volumes (especially those claiming to reveal the secrets of
personality) should be boldly marked POISON and an antidote
or vomitory prescribed to be taken after reading. For the
guidance of the reader, I suggest that this book should be
read with ten grains of salt, one for each chapter.'[1]

## Law and the Psychiatrist

Allowing one grain of salt for this quotation from his
Preface I should say that it describes fairly accurately the
mind of the legal profession in regard to the value of

[1] *Humanistic Psychology*, Preface.

psychology to a court of law. In any case, a good lawyer has little difficulty in conveying Cohen's description to a jury.

Nevertheless, modern psychotherapy's analysis of the motivations of human and criminal behaviour is the best instrument we have today for the understanding of the psychology of the criminal act. The cry of the psychiatrist from Isaac Ray of America to Dr Henry Yellowless in his Pelican volume *To Define True Madness* is that punishment should fit the man, not the crime. No doubt there is some truth in the cry that the court is too eager to administer the law, and sometimes forgetful that it is also a court of justice where justice is not only done but seen to be done. On the other hand, Granville Williams contends that: 'If there is serious criticism of the present system it is not so much because it leads to the conviction of the innocent as because in some respects it too readily assists in the acquittal of the guilty.' It is this latter danger that makes the lawyer suspect the psychologist.[1]

A court of law has two basic functions: it has to prove whether or not the crime was committed by the accused; and it has to assess the measure of responsibility and culpability for what he has done if he is proved guilty. The conflict between psychiatrist and lawyer ranges round the latter function. The state of the man's mind when he committed the act, argues the psychiatrist, must be the final factor in assessing responsibility and culpability. How far that is true we must return to later.

Now, the lawyer is not primarily concerned as to whether the accused experiences guilt-feelings or not. Indeed if he does not feel the evil of suffering, that is often taken as a sign of the accused's criminal nature. The lawyer is concerned primarily with the objective fact: Did the prisoner commit the act on which he is charged? If so, then he is guilty. But guilt in this sense must not be equated with responsibility or culpability. If the problem of guilt involved no more than that of proving whether the accused did or did not the act, then the task of the lawyer would be comparatively easy. But

[1] Hamlyn Lecture: 'The Proof of Guilt'.

it is not so simple as that. Culpability and responsibility also have to be proved, or the lack of responsibility has to be proved by the defence, if such a plea is entered. The now accepted concept of 'diminished responsibility' implies that there are gradations of responsibility; so also does the law relating to children under a certain age who are not supposed to be able to envisage the 'nature or quality' of the act.

## The McNaghten Rules

How does the court assess responsibility in a criminal charge? In Britain and America that court is largely bound by what is known as the McNaghten Rules.[1] These rules date from 1843, and were the answer to questions given to the judges of England by the House of Lords. The occasion for the questions arose out of the murder of Mr Edward Drummond, the private secretary of Sir Robert Peel, by a man called McNaghten who shot Drummond mistaking him for Sir Robert Peel. McNaghten was found to be suffering from delusions of persecution and was held not to be responsible for his actions.

The Rules formulated so long ago are still the guiding principles of the judges in criminal cases; but as a rule, they are liberally treated. The wording of the Rules tends to vary, and I qoute Zilboorg's rendering of Rule one.

'To establish a defence on the grounds of insanity, it must be clearly proved that at the time of committing the act the party accused was labouring under such defect of reason from disease of the mind as not to know the nature and quality of the act he was doing, or if he did it, that he did not know he was doing wrong.'

Dr Stafford-Clark emphasizing the second Rule expresses it in this way:

'The second important provision is that if the accused commits the act by reason of delusion, the degree of responsibility which must be attached to him, and therefore in law the degree of culpability which must be attributed, is based upon

---

[1] Cf. an interesting case where McNaghten Rule was applied in a case of Adultery, *Lancet*, June 24, 1961, pp. 1399 f.

the justification which the delusion would provide if it were true. This means that if a man suffering from schizophrenia believes that another man is killing him by electric thought waves, and kills him in self-defence he cannot be punished, although of course and properly, he will be detained in a suitable criminal hospital at Her Majesty's pleasure. If, on the other hand, the same patient's delusions were limited to the belief that his victim was depriving him of his reason and his sexual power by magical means, then, since even if this were true, it would not justify homicide in self-defence, it cannot be taken as a legitimate basis for a defence against the charge of murder, which is at present punishable by death.'[1]

Dr Stafford-Clark's comment on this latter Rule is the general opinion of psychiatrists on both sides of the Atlantic. He writes: 'In fact the law in cases of this kind makes very few mistakes. This is because the absurdity of evaluating the delusions as if they were true, and then deciding upon the degree of responsibility in which this involves the sufferer, is one which everybody recognizes.'

With that comment we can leave the second Rule out of account.

### Criticism of the Rules

How far can judge and jury assess the degree of responsibility and culpability by the application of the first Rule? Psychiatrists in America have waged a long fight against the Rule. In volume two of *The American Handbook of Psychiatry* there is a very long list of books and periodical articles dealing specifically with this question.

Psychiatrists tend to criticize the Rule as a definition of insanity which is a medical term not a legal one. It is possible, however, to approach the Rule from the angle of responsibility and culpability, and I think this is the better approach. The value of the Rule, if it has any value at all, will lie in its capacity to help the judge and jury to assess responsibility.

Criticism of the Rules has come not only from psychiatrists but from within the legal profession. Sir James Stephen away back in 1883 questioned their authority and even at that time

[1] *Psychiatry Today*, pp. 270 f.

he could write to the effect that he knew that some of the distinguished judges on the bench agreed with him. There are present-day judges of the same opinion. In America it is rather a hot question; and the Rule has been criticized by Zilboorg who spent his 'Isaac Ray Lectures' very largely in denigrating the Rule. He thought that the Rule was too intellectual and too narrow. What is meant, he asked, by the 'nature and quality of the act'? It cannot mean that the accused is supposed to know the metaphysical nature of an act. 'We must assume', he wrote, that 'by the nature of the act we mean the cruelty, the enormity, the immorality of it.' So in regard to the 'quality' of the act; here again it must mean the inhuman immorality of the act.

His main criticism, however, is that the Rule applies purely 'moralistic criteria to a clinical or scientific problem of a certain type or degree of mental disease. These moralistic criteria are the expression of man's horror of the revolting act of murder, but they are disguised in the formalistic quasi-metaphysical dress of centuries gone by which one is asked to accept as a judicial formula of logic and law. Under the circumstances, the presence of confusion is not surprising; its absence would be.'[1]

The Report of the Royal Commission on Capital Punishment was published in 1953, but one cannot say that the import of the McNaghten Rule has been essentially altered. It states that 'there is no sharp dividing line between sanity and insanity', and it did add to the 'defect of reason' 'disorders of emotions', thus recognizing such disorders as affecting one's behaviour. There was added also the Scottish concept of 'diminished responsibility'. As Zilboorg puts it: 'This is undoubtedly a step forward, or rather a *gesture* in the direction of the modern psychological knowledge of man, but it leaves the body of the McNaghten Rule almost intact, and it would add a new responsibility for the jury to discharge.'

It seems to me that the quarrel between law and psychiatry is due to the fact that the lawyer must be able to speak of guilt in objective terms, in terms of the deed of which the

[1] *Psychology of the Criminal Act*, pp. 16 f.

prisoner is accused; whereas the psychologist wants to define guilt in purely psychological terms. To the lawyer guilt attaches to the illegal act—just as the moralist attaches it to some dereliction of duty or the theologian to the violation of the law of God.

## Are There Uncontrollable Impulses?

What we must take account of is the fact that apart from mental defectives, few of those who commit crimes *but* are aware that their act is wrong in the sense that it is against the law. Even the young child knows that its naughtiness is disapproved. It is in these cases where the effects of unconscious motives inhibit the natural moral controls, and indeed seem to blot out the normal moral insight, that the McNaghten Rule fails to give guidance.

Take a case: a well educated woman of a fairly high social position volunteered to help in a soldier's canteen during the late war. She was not long there when she felt an impulse to pocket every sixpence that came across the counter her way. She had no need of the money, was perfectly aware of what she was doing, and that it was legally, socially and morally wrong. She put the money back the next day. But the impulse remained in spite of remorse. Finally she gave the job up.

Here we are brought up against the uncontrollable impulse. 'That which I would not do that I do. That which I would do I do not', wrote the Apostle Paul. Even a highly moral and religious self like St Paul could be coerced.

Nevertheless, no one can prove an uncontrollable impulse. It is an inference after the act. A psychiatrist can easily tell whether the accused knew what he was doing was wrong; but it is entirely beyond his power to say whether the impulse was irresistible. Even Freud himself admitted that if he studied the case backwards he could see the psychological reasons for the individual doing as he did; but if he started from the beginning he could not predict what the next step would be. Impulses can solicit, they need not govern.

My own experience with exhibitionists and even with kleptomaniacs and those with anti-social behaviour impulses was this: I found that there was nearly always a time-lag between the idea of the act coming into consciousness and the act itself. It is in that time-lag that the ideas can be repudiated and the impulse inhibited. But it would seem from the normal temptations of those who would be accounted mentally healthy that once the temptation has reached a certain degree of intensity a fall can be expected. The ego is coerced. And here the victim of temptation not only knows the end action contemplated but also what is tempting him to realize that end.

It is not so with those who are the victims of unconscious motives. The exhibitionist cannot understand why he should wish to expose himself; the woman I have mentioned had no idea as to why she should wish to take the sixpences.

A curious phenomenon arises here. Many people get compulsive ideas and phantasies. These barge into the conscious mind without rhyme or reason. But the curious thing is that they have no impulse to translate the ideas into action. I remember a woman coming in a very distressed state of mind. She had taken an early cup of tea to her husband. As she handed him the cup, quite spontaneously there came into her mind the idea: 'I hope the b . . . thing chokes him.' Yet there was no impulse to hurt him, apparently just the opposite. Many play with these spontaneous unsocial and even immoral phantasies, sexual or aggressive, with no impulse to put them into action. Why such ideas are in some idea-motor, and in others not we cannot say.

## Unconscious Motive and Crime

Naturally the court looks for the motive or intention of the crime. Were all motives and intentions conscious the task of judges and juries would at least be simplified. But when the psychiatrist speaks of unconscious motives the jury may be taken out of their depths. Nevertheless, there is no concept which has shed more light upon abnormal behaviour than that of the unconscious motive.

Take the case of the woman who was sent to me. When I asked her what she complained of she immediately replied: 'The Lord has commanded me to take a two-edged sword and slay my three children.' The mere thought caused the woman intense guilt-feelings, and added to that the fear that she might do so. There was nothing in the woman's conscious mind from which either she or I could infer that she did not love her children. The attribution of the command to the 'Lord' was simply an unconscious rationalization of the unconscious motive compulsively entering her conscious mind. Fortunately the woman was courageous enough to undergo analysis and intelligent enough to *see* during the analysis why such an idea so incongruous with her conscious life, should have erupted into her conscious mind.

That the unconscious plays a vital part in many crimes and anti-social behaviour should need little or no argument today. In the great majority of suicides the unconscious motive is the deciding factor. The influence and activity of the unconscious motive in behaviour with the allied concept of repression was one of the great contributions of Freud to the understanding of human motivation.

Apart from unconscious motives emotional disturbances from whatever cause can throw up ideas which can lead to apparently compulsive behaviour. Take a comparatively recent case. A man murdered his wife while she was asleep. He then took his children down to a small town on the south coast. After giving them a day on the beach and treating them, he gave both sleeping medicine and smothered them. He next tried to commit suicide by taking the rest of the medicine and attempting to drown himself. He failed to take his own life, and after wandering about in a distracted frame of mind for a further forty-eight hours he was arrested.

From the evidence and the man's statements he apparently had viewed his own and his family's future as utterly hopeless, and to save the family from the misery which his diseased emotions conjured up would come to them, he murdered them. From the point of view of his depressed mind, he was doing a good act.

No defence of insanity or diminished responsibility was entered, and he was hanged. On the McNaghten Rule it is difficult to see what valid defence could have been given. Yet I do not think Lord Deas would have hanged him. From the objective point of view he was undoubtedly guilty, but what about the subjective view?[1]

## American Attitude to the McNaghten Rules

The appeal to bring the law regarding the criminal act more into accord with the findings of modern psychology seems to have been much greater in America than in Britain. As recently as February 13, 1961, the *New York Times* had a column report of a bill to be presented by the State Department of Mental Hygiene. The bill is the outcome of three years' study by psychiatrists and lawyers of the effects of mental illness on criminal acts. It seeks chiefly 'to shelve the yard-stick' of the McNaghten Rule as to whether the defendant can 'tell right from wrong'.

Urging the use of modern penology and psychiatry to evaluate defence claims of insanity, proposals headed for the Legislature will stress the need for these steps in such cases:

1. The mental illness of the defendant should be stated as scientific findings permit.

2. It should be shown how the illness could influence the defendant's actions.

Two bills are to be presented. One seeks 'to redefine insanity and criminal responsibility along more modern lines than the old rule that fixes responsibility on the defendant's ability to 'know right from wrong', and that defines insanity as the inability to know the difference.

'The Compassion bill to amend the Code of Criminal Proceedings broadens the admissibility of psychiatric testimony in criminal trials in pleas of insanity.

'It provides that a psychiatrist who has examined a defendant be allowed to give in court a complete report of all his findings. Under present procedures such testimony can be omitted if objections against it are sustained by the court.'[2]

There are already States in which the McNaghten Rule has

---

[1] *Psychiatry Today*, p. 271.    [2] *New York Times.*

been modified by the admission of 'irresistible impulse'. New Hampshire seems to have been the first State to modify the famous Rule. What is known as the Durham Rule does not explicitly refer to criminal intent, and states the Rule in the following sentence: 'Our traditions also require that where such acts stem from and are the product of mental disease or defect, as those terms are used herein, moral blame shall not attach and hence there will not be criminal responsibility.'

Perhaps the strongest utterance against the McNaghten tradition was made by the late Mr Justice Cardozo, one of the great students of the law. He criticized vigorously 'the defective and unreal psychology underlying the McNaghten Rule' and added: 'If insanity is not to be a defence, let us say so—but let us not mock ourselves with a definition that palters with reality.'

### Oliver Wendell Holmes and Capital Punishment

That broad attitude is not characteristic of all American lawyers. Nevertheless, they have travelled a good distance from the attitude of the late Oliver Wendell Holmes as shown in a letter to the late Harold Laski. Laski had been telling him of a debate between a Dr Hyslop, a well-known psychiatrist, and Travers Humphreys, a famous criminal lawyer, on Criminal Responsibility. Apparently the lawyer had the best of the argument.

'The medicals spoke passionately of "uncontrollable impulses" and such like; Humphreys always drove them back to the vital point of getting definitions which could be explained by a judge to the average jury, and I thought he showed admirably that the refinements of psychological analysis are not yet ripe for legal use.'[1]

Holmes reply was:

'As to your doctors and judges on uncontrollable impulses, I think the short answer is that the law establishes certain minima of social conduct that a man must conform to at his peril. Of course it bears most hardly on the least prepared

[1] Quoted by Zilboorg, *Psychology of Criminal Act*, pp. 3-5.

for it, but that is what it is for. I am entirely impatient of any but broad distinctions. Otherwise we are lost in a maze of determinism.' [1]

Justice Holmes went on to say that if he were to have a talk with a man he had condemned to the electric chair he would say:

'I don't doubt your act was inevitable for you; but to make it avoidable by others we propose to sacrifice you to the common good. You may regard yourself as a soldier dying for his country if you like. But the law must keep its promises.' [2]

The curious thing about this quotation is that thirty years earlier the same Holmes gave a lecture on *Learning and Science* in which he said:

'The law, so far as it depends on learning, is indeed, as it has been called, the government of the living by the dead. To a very considerable extent no doubt it is inevitable that the living should be so governed. The past gives us our vocabulary and fixes the limits of our imagination; we cannot get away from it. There is, too, a peculiar logical pleasure in making manifest the continuity between what we are doing and what has been done before. But the present has a right to govern itself so far as it can; and it ought always to be remembered that historic continuity with the past is not a duty, it is only a necessity. "I hope that the time is coming when this thought will bear fruit. An ideal system of law should draw its postulates and its legislative justification from science. As it is now, we rely upon tradition or vague sentiment, or the fact that we never thought of any other way of doing things, as our only warrant for rules which we enforce with much confidence as if they embodied revealed wisdom. Who here can give reasons of any different kind for believing that half the criminal law does not do more harm than good?" ' [3]

One wonders what caused such a complete change of mind.

[1] Ibid.                                  [2] Ibid.
                    [3] Ibid, p. 3.

Was it that as a judge he found little in psychological science to clarify the concept of responsibility? Or was it that he became obsessed, as many judges do, with the idea of imposing sentences, not that would fit either man or crime, but to deter others?

Be that as it may, his letter brings up two points which need discussion here.

1. Does a deterrent sentence deter? It is very difficult to say. Statistics would seem to be against the inference. On the other hand, the law acts upon us as an alter Super-ego, that is it does consciously and unconsciously deepen our natural fear of consequences. We can count those who commit crimes which the ferocious sentences were supposed to deter; but we cannot count those who resist crime because they fear the evil consequences.

2. Apart altogether from the question whether deterrent sentences deter others, there is a moral problem involved. Is the law morally justified in punishing a man in order to deter others from committing the same crime? Has the accused not a big enough penalty to pay for his crime without having to suffer more to prevent others from imitating him? Is he not being punished for something for which he is not guilty?

3. But Holmes opens up the vexed question of Determinism. There is a great deal of confused thought about the doctrine of psychological determinism to which we shall give greater consideration when we treat of Ethics and Guilt.

*Lady Wootton on Mental Disorders and Criminal Responsibility*

Lady Wootton in her *Social Science and Social Pathology* has an excellent chapter on 'Mental Disorders and Criminal Responsibility' in which she quotes Dr Eliot Slater to the effect: 'No theory of mental medicine could develop without the working hypothesis of determinism.' The 'free will', according to him 'on which both law and religion are based, proves a heuristically sterile idea. If we attempt to inject it into our analysis of causation it only introduces an element of the unknowable. Statements about the responsibility of people are, moreover, really statements about the speaker's own state of mind.'[1]

We shall find this point of view shared by some moral philosophers. To them our normal judgments are simply the expression of our own state of mind.

## Psychological Determinism

What actually does psychological determinism mean? Already we have seen that behaviour is by no means predictable. It cannot then be behaviour which is determined. What I believe to be determined is what comes into our conscious mind. That is determined by the tensions, the sentiments, the character-trends, the hungers and needs of the organism and personality. We have no control of what *can* enter the conscious mind.

Control begins in consciousness. To take a simple illustration: if someone asks me: What is the name of the first woman who comes into your mind? the response is determined either by past experience or future hopes. But there is no compulsion to tell the name. I may set up a conscious resistance to revealing my interest in one. My resistance is determined by some motive, just as the name was stimulated to enter my mind by some tension the request aroused. Freud recognized this capacity to resist consciously, and warned his patients in the first interview that the success and length of treatment depended on their overcoming resistance to their free associations. How were they to overcome the resistance except on the assumption that they *could* and *ought* to? Freedom not only involves the capacity or the liberty to do something; it also involves the capacity or *the liberty not to do something*. In other words we can choose the motives which determine our actions. The Self is an agent not a billiard ball. Indeed both the practice and the theory of psychoanalysis or psychotherapy imply that the task of the analyst is to make the unconscious conscious, on the assumption that in consciousness our motives and impulses are controlled.

[1] p. 246.

The confusion lies in the fact that determinism, as Dr Slater translates it, is not determinism but pre-determinism. Behaviour may be contingent and not necessarily necessitated. Slater's tacit assumption, whether he realizes it or not, is that consciousness is always under the control of the unconscious. But as Macmurray has pointed out: 'If the theory is true then the practice must be impossible. If the practice is possible then the theory cannot be true.'[1] All that psychological determinism means is that there is no behaviour without a motive or a cause; and the Self as agent is a cause, indeed some would contend is the ultimate cause; and that it can transcend the ego.

The essential problem for law is: Could the accused have done other than he did? Determinists argue that his character being what it is he could not have done otherwise and is therefore not responsible nor culpable. Granted that his character was such that he could not have done otherwise, does that relieve him of responsibility? Is he not responsible for his character? Indeed a true evaluation of psychoanalysis theory would seem to increase our responsibility rather than lessen it.

We may even go further. Granted that there is a defect of reason because of emotional disturbance, how far is the accused responsible for the very disturbance which it is held should absolve him from responsibility? That is both a legal and a moral problem. When a man commits murder when he is drunk he is still held responsible. He is responsible for the condition in which he lost control of his behaviour. To be just to psychoanalysis the moral problem is more and more being recognized and faced. We have already seen in writings of Drs Winnicott and Bowlby that the awakening of the sense of responsibility is a matter of spontaneous growth. Nevertheless, unless there is effort on the part of the individual there is no development. The late Dr Karen Horney puts it:

'The problem of morality is again different when we believe that inherent in man are evolutionary forces which urge him to realize his given potentialities. This belief does not mean

[1] *Boundaries of Science*, p. 205.

that man is essentially good—which would presuppose a given knowledge of what is good and bad. It means that man, by his very nature and of his own accord, strives towards self-realization, and that his set of values evolve from such striving. Apparently he cannot, for example, develop his full potentialities unless he is truthful to himself, unless he is active and productive, unless he relates himself to others in the spirit of mutuality. Apparently he cannot grow if he indulges in a "dark idolatry of the self" (Shelley) and consistently attributes all his shortcomings to the deficiencies of others. He can grow, in the true sense, only if he assumes responsibility for himself.'

If that does not imply some kind of moral freedom, and man's responsibility for his character, I do not know what does. In whatever degree psychoanalytical theory implies determinism its practice demands freedom; indeed its object may be said to free the patient from his self-imprisonment, and to give him control over his responses to whatever enters his conscious mind from the unconscious. In other words to make him more conscious of his motives so as to bring them under conscious control. 'The task of therapy', wrote Dr Nunberg in *Psychoanalysis Today*,[1] 'is to mobilize the energies of the id, to make the super-ego more tolerant, and to help the ego regain its synthetic and sublimating functions as well as its own function of undisturbed perception and purposeful action.' Put that in simple terms and it means that the task of therapy is to restore the freedom which the ego has lost.

We have to return to the problem of determinism later. Meantime let us look at the grounds on which medical psychologists base their arguments for a modification of the legal concept of guilt. According to Lady Wootton writing on the implications underlying the role of mental disorder in anti-social behaviour, they seem to rest on a series of closely related propositions. First: 'It is postulated that mental health and its correlative, mental illness, are objective in the sense that they are more than expressions of the tastes and value judgments of psychiatrists or of cultural norms of

[1] p. 57.

a particular society; mental health is to be regarded as closely analogous to, and no less real, than its physical counterpart. Second, it is presumed to be possible both in theory and also (even if not always precisely) in practice, to diagnose these objective conditions of mental illness or defectiveness by criteria which are independent of any anti-social behaviour on the part of those who suffer from them; so that social persons can be divided into two classes of those who are mentally disordered, and those who are not thus handicapped. Third, the presence of mental disorder when established, is held to explain certain socially unacceptable aberrations in the sense that these are deemed to be attributable to the disorder; while fourthly, the peculiar behaviour of the mentally sick is not only explained, but also to some degree excused by their sickness. Mental illness is thus held, at least in some circumstances, to diminish if not wholly to abrogate moral responsibility; and it is widely argued also that it ought to carry with it a corresponding freedom from legal responsibility. At the same time, as mental illness is not coterminous with, nor to be defined in terms of manifestations of socially unacceptable behaviour, it follows that it is only the behaviour of some and not of all deviants that is explicable or excusable in this way.'

Are these grounds sound enough to justify the abrogation of moral and legal responsibility? Granted that mental illness is a psychological disease, is it really analogous to or as objective as physical disease? Certainly, when the mental symptoms are due to brain lesions, there can be no question of analogy; we are dealing with an objective physical disease. And law makes provision for such sufferers; even the McNaghten Rules do that. We get a verdict of 'Guilty but Insane' or one of 'diminished responsibility'.

But is there any psychological disease into which subjective factors do not enter? Is that not implicit in Freud's warning to patients about overcoming resistances to disclosing their free associations? Does he not spend pages in telling us of all the tricks by which the patients shirk the rigours of analysis? Psychological disease is a flight from reality—a subjective flight. Already I have hinted that many patients are responsible for their illness. What we find is that many acts of aggression are preceded by a long period of indulgence of phantasies of an aggressive or sexual kind which weakened and ultimately undermined the sense of moral responsibility and weakened the character by lowering the social barriers. On the other hand the illness may be an escape from the indulged phantasies because fear had been aroused that they might pass into action and be followed by the dire consequences of the law or guilt-feelings.

## Failure to Define a Concept of Mental Health

Apart from these considerations, it is doubtful if we can equate mental disease with physical illness. The correlative of mental illness is mental health. But this is a very difficult thing to define as anyone will find if they read through Lady Wootton's chapter on 'Social Pathology and the Concept of Mental Health'. Psychiatrists, so far, have not been able to produce a concept either of mental illness or of mental health in 'objective scientific terms that are free from subjective moral terms'. The whole subject becomes more complicated if we try to define mental health or illness in terms of personality. This is what Dr Guirdham, a psychiatrist of Bath, in his *A Theory of Disease* sets out to do. The diseases with which we have to contend apart from ageing or an invasion of bacilli depend entirely on the type of personality we are. 'Proneness to disease', he writes, 'is related to the degree of development of personality. The value the individual sets on his personality stands in direct relation to his proneness to psychosomatic and neurotic disorders.' 'If I am required to summarize in a sentence what is the fundamental theme of this book I would say that, in my view, health is a by-product of religious experience. Perhaps I should qualify this by saying that, in our present state of knowledge, this conclusion should be regarded as applying chiefly to the skin diseases and neurotic disorders.'[1] Add that to the selection of definitions in Lady Wootton's chapter culled from leading psychiatrists,

[1] Preface.

all differing and laying the emphasis on different marks of mental health, and the confusion becomes worse confounded. Very largely definitions of mental health are determined by the subjectives attitudes of the psychiatrists.

## Difficulty of Relating Mental Illness to Responsibility

If mental health is difficult to define it follows that no less difficulty will be found in defining mental illness, especially the degree of responsibility and culpability the mental illness would involve. I agree with the psychiatrists that it is not for the judge to define either mental health or mental illness, but it is his duty and his alone to assess responsibility. To quote Dr Henry Yellowlees, a frequent witness in criminal cases where the state of mind of the accused is in question, 'Doctors are painfully slow and unwilling to realize that the last word on the question of criminal responsibility, just as on the question of guilt or innocence, must rest with the law, and must also be seen to rest with the law, and that no rule will ever be framed, or any procedure ever conceived, which will make medical men the final arbiters on the question of criminal responsibility. That legal question must be settled by judge and jury alone.[1]

Granted that mental illness is an entity, what degree of mental illness absolves a wife-beater? The shop lifter? The bank robber? The killer? Are we to go the whole hog and contend that criminality is a disease and thus get rid of the concept of guilt altogether? Not a few psychiatrists, as Lady Wootton shows are aware of this danger, and indeed of the fallacy of equating crime and disease. She quotes with approval the late Sir Norwood East's dictum that 'as a result of more than fifty years practical experience of crime I am unable to regard crime as a disease, although sometimes the result of it.' So also Dr Desmond Curran who said: 'It is absurd to maintain that an unhappy man is necessarily sick . . . or that a delinquent man is necessarily sick. The decision as to whether a man is sick or not does not purely depend upon unhappiness, inefficiency or social inadequacy as such.'[2]

[1] Quoted by Lady Wootton, p. 227.　　　　[2] Ibid.

But there is the other side. There are those who like Dr Eliot Slater, quoted by Lady Wootton, who rejects the idea of responsibility. He contends: 'No theory of mental medicine could develop without the working hypothesis of determinism'. 'Free will', he believes, injected into the theory of causation, introduces an element of the unknowable. The unknowable here can mean nothing else than the unpredictable. Not only so but he seems to think of 'free will' as an entity acting arbitrarily in its own right. Not only does he seem to be confusing between the unknowable and the unpredictable, but his use of the term 'determinism' is really equivalent to 'pre-determinism'. No one will deny that every act has a cause and is determined by it; I cannot think there is such a thing as causeless behaviour in humans any more than there is a causeless event in physics. 'Free will' is the capacity of the Self both to choose between alternatives and to canalize its energy towards a self-chosen end, and to inhibit action inconsistent with that end. Complexes, sentiments, character structures, even phobias can solicit the Self, but they need not govern. Is not the final aim of mental medicine to help the patient to choose differently? When an individual in virtue of analysis realizes the cause of his anti-social behaviour—and this is not confined to criminal behaviour—it is then up to him to choose a different motive from which to act; in other words to respond in a different way to his complexes, sentiments or neurotic character structures. We are 'determined' but not pre-determined. The Self is not a football kicked towards this goal or that, the helpless victim of opposing impulses; it is the controller of the game.

I shall be confronted with the concept of 'motiveless behaviour' or the psychopath. That there are crimes and behaviour of an anti-social kind which seem to have no motive no one will deny. But we cannot infer from our ignorance that there is no motive; the motive may be unconscious, or it may be anti-sociality itself. To admit motiveless behaviour is to introduce a surd into behaviour which cannot be resolved.

## The Psychopath

The psychopath presents a different problem and a difficult one. Mentally and from the point of view of intelligence he is not defective. He is infantile in the sense that he has remained ego-centric to the *n*th degree. Neither the negative nor the positive conscience has been awakened or it has been entirely repressed. He has never become what Dr Waddington terms an 'ethical animal'. But the fact that he experiences no guilt-feelings does not absolve him from objective guilt. How far physical causes account for his condition it is difficult to say. Dr Stafford-Clark tells us that psychopaths 'display a pattern of electrical activity in their brain, recorded by a special instrument, which has come to be recognized as evidence of immature functions and resembles that normally seen only in children. Another line of study which recently has led to a striking contribution towards the recognition of the physical characteristics of the psychopath has been the study of the formation of capillary loops in the nail bed. These again show immature forms in a significantly high proportion of cases.'[1]

It is not contended that these physical characteristics account for the psychopath's mental characteristics of emotional immaturity; his fecklessness, rootlessness and infidelity. They are aware of their condition and indeed most of them are unhappy about it. A pathological liar knows he is lying though he may not know why he should lie when truth-telling would seem to serve him better. Granted that he is no more responsible for his condition than the homosexual, that would not necessarily absolve him from guilt, no more than a homosexual is absolved from homosexual practices which might corrupt others. He may have no moral feelings, no more than the child has whose 'pattern of electrical activity' is similar. Nevertheless he is well aware that he is acting contrary to conventional standards of behaviour and he knows the law just as a child knows what is approved and not approved by the parents. It is doubtful if anyone could prove that he could not have acted differently.

[1] Ibid. p. 117.

Mr Goodhart has contended that obedience to the law is based neither upon fear nor upon coercion:

'The strength of English Law, from the basic rules of the constitution to the minor regulations issued by a local authority depends in large part on the fact that the people of this country recognize that they are under an obligation to obey the law, and that this sense of obligation is based, not upon force or fear, but on reason, morality and religion and the inherited traditions of the nation. It is for this reason that we can truly say that the common law is our common heritage.'[1]

It is this sense of obligation on which law is based that seems to be defective in the psychopath. There is unquestioned diminished responsibility. He is admittedly the most difficult type of person to treat by psychotherapy. And if Dr Hadfield is right that the lack of a moral sense is constitutional then nothing apparently can be done about it. Hadfield found that in the Services where discipline is much stricter than in civilian life nothing could be done with him, and he was discharged. A differential diagnosis between the psychopath and the rebel, whose rebellion is the outcome of upbringing, is sometimes difficult to make. Heavy sentences protect the public but they do not deter this type of anti-social individual.

*Psychiatrists have not Produced a Criterion of Responsibility*

From the study of legal guilt I cannot but think that although the psychiatrists have made a good case for the modification of the McNaghten Rules they have not produced criteria by which a judge and jury could assess the degree of responsibility or culpability. Both lawyers and medical psychologists know that the McNaghten Rules are unsatisfactory in spite of many attempts to modify them. Simply to cut the Gordian knot by equating crime with disease and thus undermine the concept of responsibility is unlikely to be acceptable either to medicine or law. As we have seen, and Dr Yellowlees admits, judges interpret the Rules very liberally. He gives one excellent instance of the summing up of a case

[1] *English Law and Moral Law*, p. 151.

where a plea of insanity was entered: 'Early in the course (of the summing up) the Judge said:

"Whereas the burden is on the Prosecution to prove that the Accused did the acts complained of, that burden is a very strict one; they have on that issue, to satisfy you beyond reasonable doubt. But when the burden, as here, is on the Defence to prove insanity in law, they do not have to satisfy you beyond reasonable doubt; it is sufficient if they satisfy you that on the balance of probabilities he was insane. It is sufficient for them, if, at the end of the case, you can say, looking at all the facts: we think it is probable that at the time he was insane."

'He returned to the point in his closing sentence, which was:

"You will remember always that you do not have to be satisfied beyond reasonable doubt that he is insane; but merely that it is sufficient if you feel that he probably was." '[1] Verdict: Guilty but insane.

Here in Britain we have one safeguard against the possibility of one with diminished responsibility being sent to the gallows. In every case where a plea of insanity has been entered and not allowed the accused is then subjected to expert examination after conviction. Legal criteria of responsibility and laws of evidence cease to hamper an unbiased conclusion, 'indeed the examination is very strongly coloured with that humanity which is traditional in medicine and in the law of this country, and which still adorns the practice of both professions'.[2]

Dr Yellowlees's own solution is that Crown and Defence: 'Should call as many psychiatrist witnesses as they care, but let these witnesses consult together and bring in, if humanly possible, an agreed report for the jury to accept—or reject, if they have the hardihood, the folly to do so—rather than have their differences exploited in court to the confusing of the issue, the darkening of counsel with words, the degrading

[1] *To Define True Madness*, p. 151.
[2] Ibid. p. 152.

of noble speciality, and the sad lowering of the dignity of both professions.'[1]

That seems reasonable and would certainly do away with the badgering to which the psychiatrist is subjected by a clever prosecuting counsel.

## The Assessment of Responsibility must Remain with the Law

To sum up: the present position seems to be that intellectual, rigid, and too narrow as the McNaghten Rules are in the light of modern psychological knowledge of human motivation we have nothing better to put in their place. Lady Wootton does not go too far when after a thorough examination of the whole problem of Mental Illness and Criminal Responsibility she concludes:

'Once we allow any movement away from a rigid intellectual test of responsibility on McNaghten lines, our feet are set upon the slippery slope which offers no real resting place short of abandonment of the whole concept of responsibility. . . . Already in many countries, amongst which England must now be included, the first steps down the slope have been taken; and the possibility cannot be dismissed that the relaxation of the definition of responsibility which is already in progress is the beginning of a process which, in the remote future, is destined to result in the total destruction of the concept itself.'[2]

We have seen how the State Department of Mental Hygiene in America seems to be moving that way, and if the bill to be presented to the legislature were to be passed I think we would be well on the slippery slope.

After all, the psychiatrists cannot have the last word in the assessing of responsibility. They are trained to understand and to describe the state of mind of the accused; but when it comes to assessing responsibility it is difficult to get two psychiatrists to agree. Psychotherapy is not an exact science, indeed it is an art rather than a science. Intuition and empathy, to say nothing of 'hunches' are not the least active

[1] Ibid. p. 148 f.
[2] *Social Science and Social Pathology*, p. 249.

factors in the psychotherapist's art of probing the mental processes of his patients. The quotation from Cohen is not a caricature of psychology; it simply indicates how far we are from an exact science of human behaviour. No two individuals are the same. There is that element of individuality which plays havoc with the scientific aim of bringing every individual instance under some general principle. The predictability of behaviour is never more than a probability; it is an inference from habit, and what we have been accustomed to do in the past. But who is to predict whether the ingrained habit is to be broken? Have we not seen alcoholics without help from anyone suddenly break with their old ways and resume a life of abstinence and social respectability? Their behaviour is still determined but new motives have been chosen and new values sought. The recognition of responsibility for one's behaviour and one's character, the willingness to accept guilt-feelings arising from objective guilt is the sign of a developing moral character, and one of the first steps to mental health.

## Law and the Moral Law

I have already quoted A. L. Goodhart, Q.C., to the effect that the obligation to obey the law of the land is rooted in our moral nature. We may grant that there are many who are kept from running foul of the law from fear of the consequences. They fear the law rather than respect it; but even these may feel that if they break the law their punishment is deserved. There are others who defy the law; but their very defiance is the sign that it has its grip on the unconscious mind. The guilt-feelings experienced when we break the law must come from those moral roots on which the law of the land is based.

It does not follow that the law is perfect. It has many anomalies as Mr Goodhart has pointed out and given excellent examples. But the anomalies themselves are recognized through our moral insight into justice; and the claim that unjust laws be changed is based on the assumption that the law is moral.

Thus it would seem that the guilt-feelings are not imposed by the law; they do not arise because we have broken the law but because we have wounded our own moral nature by our anti-social behaviour.

This brings up a very interesting problem. We are accustomed to think that the present outbreak of crime is the outcome of an upsurge of defiance of the law. Does this go deep enough? If Goodhart is right in his contention that the obligation to keep the law is rooted in our moral nature then could it not be that the real root of anti-social behaviour is due to the degeneration of our moral nature? If our moral nature is degenerating then it follows that the basis for the respect for the law and the very foundation on which the keeping of the law rests must be weakened. The aggressive impulses, and the ego-centricity from which all crime proceeds are lacking those inner controls without which the law is ignored rather than defied. The sense of guilt is not merely the result of wrong-doing but a protector from wrong-doing. The Super-ego tends to threaten us before we have done wrong; and indeed can, in one in whom it has been developed, repress the evil tendencies and cause a flight into psychological disease to prevent the violation of its 'musts' and 'must-nots'. The function of the Super-ego is to prevent us from violating what is socially and morally approved. With the decay of religion, the lack of parental discipline, the feebleness of ethical teaching, the Super-ego even if to some degree elicited, never gains the strength to restrain the aggressive and ego-centred impulses. Guilt-feelings never become strong enough to be a controlling factor in the obeying of the law.

Actually the law is the objectified Super-ego; but if the subjective Super-ego is undeveloped then there is nothing in the personality to which the law can appeal.

Here, then is a problem for the criminologist, the psychologist, the moralist and our religious teachers. There are writers who want to get rid of the concept of guilt altogether; to them guilt-feelings are the evil thing. They do not seem to realize that the capacity for guilt-feelings is the strongest, even the ultimate, basis for complying with the law. Granted that the Super-ego is to make us fear evil and the law rather than to love the good, nevertheless, even in the individual with a mature conscience, it is still active in so far as it makes him stop and think when the moral issues of moral choice are confused.

### SELECTED BOOKS

*The Juridical Review.* August/December, 1959.

*English Law and the Moral Law.* A. L. Goodhart, K.B.E., Q.C., Hamlyn Lectures, published by Stevens.

*Psychology of the Criminal Act and Punishment.* Gregory Zilboorg, M.D., London, Hogarth Press.

*Psychiatry and Law.* Guttmacher and Weihoven, New York, Norton.

*Social Science and Social Pathology.* Barbara Wootton, London, George Allen & Unwin.

*Psychiatry Today.* D. Stafford Clark, London, Pelican Books.

# CHAPTER 4

# ETHICS AND GUILT

We have already seen in the quotation from Professor Lewis that moral philosophers have tended to shirk the problem of guilt, in spite of the fact that guilt 'is first and foremost an ethical problem'.

*Different Theories of the Subject Matter of Ethics*

The real difficulty for the outsider is to know just exactly what the subject matter of Ethics is; and what moral judgments connote, or whether they connote anything at all. If I turn to the late Professor Laird I read: 'The problem which moral enquiry has to consider is whether any given action is what it ought to be. In other words, moral theory is concerned with the reasons that justify action; or else condemn it. What is asked is whether there are any such reasons and if so, how and in what degree they justify.' Laird saw Ethics as 'the justification of imperatives'. The content of the ought, the command, which the ought implies, must be justified.[1]

If I turn to Rashdall I find that

'Ethics . . . deals with the Nature of morality . . . with what we mean or ought to mean by these terms—what is the meaning and nature of "good" and "right". Moral philosophy is a science which deals with all the questions raised about good and right. In particular it will be found that the general question breaks itself up into three main enquiries: .

'1. What is the general nature of good and evil, right and wrong—what at bottom do we mean when we pronounce such and such a thing to be good, and such and such an action to be right?

'2. Assuming there is some real meaning in the terms, that

87

they do correspond to some real distinction in the nature of things the question arises, "By what part of our nature do we recognize these distinctions? What at bottom are the judgments that we usually call moral judgments? Are they merely attempts to express in words a particular kind of feeling or emotion, or are they a specific kind of intellectual judgment? Or are they neither the one nor the other—neither feeling nor thought nor any combination of the two, but something absolutely *sui generis*?"

'3. Granting that we know in a general way what we mean by calling an act right or wrong, there arises the further question: "How can we find out what particular acts are right or wrong? . . . This is generally known as the question of the Moral Criterion."

'Dr A. C. Ewing taking account of linguistic analysis describes Ethics in this way: "Ethics is concerned with two main kinds of question, first with deciding the general principles on which ethical terms, i.e. good, bad, duty, etc., are to be applied to anything; secondly with deciding precisely what these terms mean." ' [1]

This is undoubtedly a popular description, and scarcely brings out the idea in his other volumes that for him as for Laird and Hastings 'the fundamental concept of Ethics is *ought*'. But it includes the modern preoccupation with the meaning of ethical terms. Each of these authors lays the emphasis upon *ought* as an ultimate notion; the right is something that ought to be done, and by implication the failure to obey the ought, to forward the good, to choose the wrong when the choice of the right was possible to us is to incur objective guilt. 'Guilt', according to Professor Lewis, 'is some betrayal of what I take to be my duty by which my conduct becomes directly morally evil and blameworthy.'

'The conditions of guilt are therefore precisely the same as the conditions of moral evil, but we must not allow the notion of guilt to drop out in considering the nature and conditions

[1] *Ethics*, p. 1. *Second Thoughts in Moral Philosophy*, p. 5.

of moral evil, for we shall then be inclined to overlook the peculiarity of moral evil as so many moral philosophers have done, and assimilate it to other forms of evil which do not presuppose a special kind of wrongdoing and do not expose us to blame.'[1]

One could multiply names of philosophers to whom guilt, by implication at least, is an objective reality; that is, it does not simply refer to subjective feelings of approbation or disapprobation, but to human conduct, and to conduct for which the agent is responsible and blameworthy. Indeed, it is from this point of view that Sir David Ross takes his starting point in his *Foundations of Ethics*. He starts with the fact of the moral consciousness, the fact that we believe that there is 'the existence of a large body of beliefs and convictions to the effect that there are certain kinds of acts that ought to be done, and certain kinds of things that ought to be brought into existence'.[2]

That surely implies that if we violate what ought to be done, or fail to bring some good into existence when we have the opportunity, we are guilty.

Professor Broad contends that we know or believe that we ought to keep promises and that we know it to be wrong to inflict useless pain.

Could we stop there little difficulty would be found in coming to the conclusion that, like legal guilt, moral guilt is an objective fact. Alas! we cannot stop there. To all these philosophers I have mentioned the judgments of conscience are judgments of reason, and not simply of feeling, although guilt-feelings may be generated by the objective guilt.

## Protest Against Theological Hedonism

I do not think it would be untrue to say that the emphasis upon the feeling side of conscience came as a protest against what Rashdall calls 'theological hedonism', or what Bradley called 'The do it or be damned' theory of ethics! That the protest was justified is evidenced by a story told by Rashdall

[1] *Morals and Revelation*, p. 158.
[2] Quoted by P. H. Nowell-Smith, *Ethics*, p. 5.

worth recounting. Francis Hutcheson, who like Shaftesbury attempted to defend the disinterestedness of moral motive against those who based moral obligation solely on the fear of Hell and the hope of Heaven, was an earnest Presbyterian minister—liberal according to the standard of his time, but sincerely theistic and Christian. He preached one Sunday for his father who also was a Presbyterian minister. On the latter's return to his manse, he was greeted by the orthodox elder:

'We a' feel muckle wae for your mishap, Reverend Sir, but it cannot be concealed. Your silly loon, Frank, has fashed a' the congregation wi' his idle cackle, for he has been babbling this 'oor aboot a gude and benevolent God, and that the sauls of the heathen themselves will gang to heaven if they follow the licht o' their ain conscience. Not a word does the daft boy ken, speer nor say aboot the gude auld comfortable doctrine o' election, reprobation, original sin and faith. Hoot man awa' wi' sic a fellow.'[1]

Rashdall's condemnation of the theory is that it reduces conscience to nothing but 'a comfortable feeling', and blurs the distinction between good and evil.

## Hume and Ayer

But the true precursor of modern subjectivism and the emotional theory of ethics, was David Hume. Indeed, Ayer acknowledges that his doctrines are 'themselves the logical outcome of the empiricism of Berkeley and David Hume'.[2] To Hume moral ideas and judgments were simply feelings of approbation or disapprobation. What is socially approved is good and right. He had the curious notion of likening the good moral feelings to those which a poor man was likely to have for the rich and well-fed, well dressed, and well looked after rich man, whereas the bad feelings were the kind of contempt or disgust the rich might have for the poor, unkempt man—'an apotheosis of flunkeyism'.

Naturally there is a great deal more in Hume's moral theory; but here we are concerned only with the problem of

[1] "Is Conscience an Emotion?" p. 12 f.
[2] Language, Truth and Logic. Preface to First edition.

guilt. It is difficult to see how there could be any such thing as objective guilt if conscience is a matter of subjective feelings. No doubt subjective 'guilt'-feelings would be experienced by someone who had transgressed what was approved by convention or his own sense of right or wrong; and the fear of punishment could certainly be painful if the individual were faced with the consequences of legal guilt. But such feelings could be lived down as often they are by those whose sense of moral responsibility is weak. For feelings of conscience to possess objectivity, they must refer to the violation of an obligation, or the reality of vicious living; they must refer to what Professor Lewis calls 'moral evil'.

To the older moral philosophers with their metaphysical outlook the terms, 'good', 'right', 'ought', 'wrong' had meaning. Not a little of recent Ethical thinking has been influenced by logical positivism, or as some have called it, 'linguistic positivism'. The chief exponent of the application of linguistical positivism to Ethics is Professor Ayer in his 'Language, Truth and Logic'. A good deal of later writing on Ethics has been inspired by this stimulating small volume.

According to his theory, only propositions of mathematics and logic definitions of symbols, and those propositions based upon observation or sense impressions can be true or false. It follows that there can be no such thing as ethical science, as ethical judgments are mere expressions of feelings. It must not be inferred that Ayer is here echoing the position of the subjectivists; he is far more radical than that, and denies that ethical statements can be either true or false; they are meaningless. His own illustration will help us here:

'The presence of an ethical symbol in a proposition adds nothing to its factual content. Thus if I say to someone: "You acted wrongly in stealing that money", I am not stating anything more than if I had simply said, "You stole that money". In adding that this action is wrong I am not making any further statement about it. I am simply evincing my moral disapproval of it. It is as if I had said "You stole that money" in a particular tone of horror, or written it with the addition of some special exclamation marks. The tone, or the exclamation marks, add nothing to the literal meaning of the sentence.'[1]

## Linguistic Position of Ayer

There can be no mistaking the Professor's meaning. Moral judgments according to this theory, are not judgments of fact; conscience expresses nothing but feeling. It must be noted, however, that Ayer allows that descriptive terms can be either true or false. He contrasts two types of ethical symbols and shows how the one use is meaningless and the other capable of verification: 'Thus a complex sign of the form, "X is wrong" may constitute a sentence which expresses a moral judgment concerning a certain type of conduct, or it may constitute a sentence which states that a certain type of conduct is repugnant to the moral sense of a particular society. In the latter case "wrong" is a descriptive ethical symbol and the sentence in which it occurs expresses a sociological proposition; in the former case, the symbol "wrong" is a normative ethical symbol, and the sentence in which it occurs does not, we maintain, express an empirical proposition at all.' Thus if a man runs foul of the law of the land he has done wrong; he has done something which the law does not allow. He has incurred a legal guilt; his guilt is objective. But to pass from that to the assertion that he has incurred moral guilt is to pass from something which is empirically obvious, to making a meaningless statement which can be neither true nor false. We should simply be expressing our feelings regarding the criminal and the crime.

Naturally, I am only concerned here with how this linguistic theory bears upon the concept of guilt. 'Stealing money is a fact'; 'Stealing money is wrong' is, according to Ayer, not a fact but a value judgment and expresses only our feelings.

But does that judgment express feelings only? Psychologically it expresses more than feelings about stealing as a fact. It expresses an interpretation of the fact, and interpretation— in this case a moral judgment—is an act of reason and not

[1] *Language, Truth and Logic*, p. 107.

merely of feeling. Are there any pure facts entirely bereft of interpretation? Do we know any empirical facts entirely bereft of interpretation? Suppose I see a blot of some kind on the paper on which I am writing; I can say 'I see a patch of colour'; but to say 'colour', indeed to say 'blot' is to interpret the fact, and in terms of sense impressions which are feelings. All perception is interpretation and before a sense impression means anything or can become a perception it needs interpretation. It seems to me that what Professor Ayer has to do is to show that my interpretation of stealing as 'wrong' is true or false; merely to assert that the term 'wrong' is an expression only of feeling is psychologically false. I have added to the fact of stealing its interpretation, as an act, in an analogous way to saying that the 'blot' is a patch of yellow colour.

If I take his statement 'X is wrong' as a descriptive ethical symbol of conduct repugnant to the moral sense of a particular society I have not reduced it to a sociological proposition. The man is condemned as guilty; but that is to say he is blameworthy, and blameworthy with its implication of responsibility is a normative ethical symbol. Otherwise, Professor Ayer must accept the position that conduct which is repugnant to a particular society simply expresses collectivized feeling.

## Emotive Theory of Ethics

Ayer's position, if I understand him aright, is that ethical statements express nothing objective, and as statements of feeling, can neither be true nor false. This is the familiar emotivist theory in its most dogmatic form. Naturally if we reduce ethical judgments to mere feelings then 'it is impossible to find a criterion for determining the validity of ethical judgments',[1] and Hastings Rashdall was all wrong in telling us that a part of ethical philosophy was to find a moral criterion. In other words there can be no such thing as objective guilt.

[1] *Language, Truth and Logic*, p. 108.

Nevertheless, Ayer allows, what Stevenson has worked out in detail,

'that ethical terms do not serve only to express feeling. They are calculated to arouse feeling, and so to stimulate action. Indeed some of them are used in such a way as to give the sentences in which they occur the effect of commands. Thus the sentence: "It is your duty to tell the truth", may be regarded both as an expression of a certain sort of ethical feeling about truthfulness and as the expression of the command "Tell the truth". The sentence "You ought to tell the truth" also involves the command, "Tell the truth", but here the tone of the command is less emphatic. In the sentence, "It is good to tell the truth" the command becomes little more than a suggestion. And the "meaning" of the word "good", in its ethical usage is differentiated from the word "duty" or the word "ought". In fact we may define the meaning of various ethical words in terms both of the different feelings they are ordinarily taken to express, and also the different responses which they are calculated to provoke.' [1]

It would seem to be a waste of time and energy to use ethical terms to arouse feeling towards some kind of action or the inhibition of action if the ethical value of that action had no objectivity, but was only an expression of feeling. But as a matter of psychological fact ethical feelings presuppose the objectivity of ethical judgments, and flow from these. Feelings are aroused by the judgment not the judgment from the feelings. The objectivity of a sense perception is a moment in its givenness. I do not infer the objectivity of my sense perceptions: it is an essential element in the experience. So the objectivity of moral judgments, e.g. that stealing is wrong is a moment in the moral perception. That does not mean that my ethical judgments are always true. The question of the validity of moral judgments is not a psychological question; that is to say that it can pass no verdict on the content of the *ought*, on what we are obliged to do or to refrain from doing; but it can say that the experience of the ought, of obligation is an irreducible

[1] *Language, Truth and Logic*, p. 108.

experience in the development of moral character and personality. Psychology can never be the basis of ethics, for the simple reason that all desires whether desirable or not, all behaviour whether considered right or wrong, all motives and sentiments be they named good or bad, are its subject matter. Psychology has no technique that could tell us what we ought to desire. Psychology can throw some light on the history of the individual's morals; it can by its exploration of the unconscious and the making of the unconscious conscious free us from moral compulsions or inhibitions, so that we get greater control over our desires and motives; it can help us to adjust to a code of ethics, but it cannot itself provide us with an ethical code. Ayer's statement that one of the 'chief causes of moral behaviour is fear, both conscious and unconscious, of a god's displeasure, and fear of the enmity of society' is to reduce all morality to Super-ego morality, as a matter of fact to 'borrowed morality'. Granted that there are many who are morally immature, granted that the 'do it or be damned' theory of ethics still governs some, it is the free acceptance of a 'rational good' which has led to our higher civilization.

To accept Ayer's theory of ethics would be to put all subjective feelings of guilt into the category of 'neurotic', unrealistic, guilt-feelings, and should mean that we all should be lying on the psychoanalyst's couch!

'Ethics, as I conceive it, is the logical study of the language of morals', writes R. M. Hare.[1] And I should think Professor Ayer would not disagree with that view, if I understand aright his foreword to Nowell-Smith's Pelican book on *Ethics*. In that foreword he writes: 'There is a distinction . . . between the activity of a moralist who sets out to elaborate a moral code, or to encourage its observance, and that of the moral philosopher whose concern is not primarily to make moral judgments but to analyse their nature.'[2] Between the moral reformer and the moral philosopher there is undoubtedly a gulf; but we can say that the moral

[1] *The Language of Morals*, p. v.
[2] *Ethics*, P. H. Nowell-Smith, Editorial Foreword.

philosopher's function is exhausted in analysing the nature of moral judgments? Surely not. The analysis of moral judgments is certainly one of his functions; but is there not the greater function of evaluating rationally our moral experience—not merely describing the phenomena of moral experience. No philosopher worth the name could possibly stop at Professor Ayer's first class of ethical propositions as the expression of 'definition of ethical terms of judgments about the legitimacy or possibility of certain definitions'. Nor would he agree with the Professor's second class that description of phenomena of moral experience—which is certainly the task of the psychologist and sociologist—is all he is concerned with. His task is to evaluate moral experience. Certainly if one starts, as Ayer does, with a definition of the verification principle which by its very nature excludes not only moral valuation but all values, then one can do no more with him than one can with the moral sceptic who denies that there is such a thing as moral obligation. 'When I choose a word', Humpty Dumpty said, in a scornful tone, 'it means just what I choose it to mean—neither more nor less.' First Ayer chooses his verification principle, and then that only will be meaningful which can be tested by it. In other words the verification becomes a dogma.

### Teaching Moral Behaviour to Children

Perhaps I may be allowed before passing to other aspects of ethics connected with the problem of guilt to use a suggestion of Hare's which shows that even he cannot just be satisfied with his own definition of ethics as dealing with the 'logical study of the language'. 'Even for me', he writes, 'it is a question of "How shall I bring up my children?"' To quote the passage from the Fellow of Balliol:

'What shall I do in such and such a situation? is almost invariably answered without ambiguity by the moral intuitions which my upbringing has given me; if I ask myself "How shall I bring up my children?" I pause before giving an answer. It is here that the most fundamental moral decision of all arises; and it is here, if only moral philosophers would pay attention to them, that the most characteristic uses of moral words are to be found.'[1]

Hare points out that we can teach principles but we cannot make decisions for our children. It is only as the growing child becomes capable of making decisions for himself that he ceases to live on 'borrowed morality'. No logical study of the language of morals will help a growing child to make decisions; to make decisions the child's sense of moral responsibility has to be awakened; he has to value morally the alternatives. Moral words have no meaning for me until I have assimilated that meaning through my moral consciousness. In other words, ethics has to do with more than the logical study of words, it has to evaluate the moral experience these words express. The meaning of moral words applies to me and my conduct. Let us apply Hare's suggestion to Ayer's theory: Am I to say to my children that 'Stealing is wrong', is meaningless and a matter of feeling? There is nothing in such a theory that could possibly elicit a sense of moral responsibility, nor could we on the theory give our children a moral criterion. If guilt is a matter of individual or social disapprobation we need to pay no attention to guilt-feelings; they could only be classed as 'neurotic'. Nevertheless, like a functional pain in the body, the neurotic feelings are a sign that something is wrong morally.

## Guilt and Ethical Responsibility

The mention of responsibility leads immediately to the relation of both subjective and objective guilt to responsibility. Guilt involves *responsible for something* and *responsibility to someone or something*. I am responsible for keeping the law, and I am responsible to society for my behaviour. Theology would contend that morality is far more than this; that we are responsible for our thoughts, emotions and behaviour to God. Moral philosophy would contend that 'when every allowance has been made for the deference we should pay to established opinions, and the claims of important social institutions, the fact remains that society like the individual

[1] *The Language of Morals*, pp. 74 f.

is fallible, and that the claims of its institutions have a limit—a limit which in some circumstances, justify open resistance'.[1]

On the other hand moral philosophers are just as emphatic that moral principles are not dependent on religious dogma. Ethics, they argue, is an autonomous discipline. 'The view we adopt', writes Lewis, 'is that mature persons have a proper awareness of moral distinctions quite independently of their adoption of any religious faith.'[2] A. C. Ewing expresses it: 'Ethics has a quite distinct character, a quite distinct logic of its own.'[3] Laird is even more emphatic: 'Morality is absolute and autonomous. It is neither cold nor unsubstantial, and its strength, psychologically speaking, is authoritative and well attested. Indeed there are solid reasons for supposing that many religions would be of little account if *they* were not "fired with morality", and when the two conflict, it is not morality which should yield.'[4]

But this lands us in a difficulty which I have not seen discussed anywhere. If morality is autonomous, and 'man's duties are given to us' as 'claims which we must fulfil, claims, which in some way are within our power, but which do not depend on our reactions and impressions (then) . . . the truth is not relative to us in ethics any more than in other spheres. Our duties exist in the nature of things and there are independent standards which we presuppose in any appraisement of men's activities.' *What then are we responsible to?*

## What Are We Ethically Responsible To?

Perhaps we can gain some insight into this problem of *responsibility to* if we examine the concept of responsibility. It implies the capacity for self-determination, and indeed some prevision of the consequences of our actions; but it also connotes the feeling of accountability, of being answerable for our thoughts, feelings and acts; to feel responsible is to experience a sense of obligation to do, think or feel something.

[1] *Morals and the New Theology*, pp. 22 f.
[2] Ibid. p. 24.
[3] *Second Thoughts in Moral Philosophy*, p. 35.
[4] *A Study in Moral Theory*, p. 326.

It is here that we have the source of guilt-feelings. How often does the psychotherapist hear a patient say: 'I blame myself.' But we need not go to the neurotic for the reference of guilt-feelings to himself. We all have known what it is to be ashamed of ourselves because we shirked some obligation, acted contrary to our moral principles, lost control of our temper or our tongue. We know that what we did was not something that happened through some accident or disease, but something we brought about. True guilt-feelings always contain a moment of the sense of responsibility, of accountability for what we did.

Does this throw light on what we are *responsible to?* Does it not hint that we are responsible to our own conscience? Conscience is the moral mirror of our very being, the mirror in which the Self which has done the guilty thing sees itself. The Self, given the responsibility for its own character, for the expression of its desires and feelings, sees its own weakness. Conscience is the synthesis of all our moral principles and moral ideas; it is the organization of all our moral motives into the moral sentiment. Our conduct has violated that sentiment, and our distressing guilt-feelings are the result.

We experience the sense of blameworthiness, and not seldom experience the desire for punishment, and indeed often resort to self-punishment in an attempt to expiate our guilt, as though it were possible to take all the consequences of what we did or what we are on our own heads. As we saw earlier guilt-feelings are the most miserable anyone can feel. Even the slightest guilt-feeling can darken the brightest day. Hence the morbid resort to repression, rationalization of our conduct and over-compensation—all these are just ways by which we attempt to ward off guilt-feelings. If the paradox can be accepted, the Self has violated the Self. *Guilt-feelings are self-generated because the Self is responsible to itself.*

### What Are We Responsible For?

To answer this question thoroughly would mean a volume on the psychology of moral action. Here I must be less ambitious.

Naturally we are not responsible for our environment unless we can change it; and that a little child cannot do at the period when environment has a great deal to do with the kind of moral habits and moral sentiments we acquire. Nevertheless, as self-consciousness grows the environment becomes no more than the opportunity for the Self to react. Sir Henry Jones in his *Working Faith of a Social Reformer* 'contended that character and environment cannot be separated: a man and his world are one'. To one man his environment may be the occasion for some inspiration for noble service, to another the opportunity for exploitation. Our moral environment, however, provides the child with the first content of its Super-ego. It begins, as we have seen, with the introjection of what is approved or disapproved; but as conscience develops, and moral insight takes the place of parental or community demands, the 'musts' and 'must-nots' of parental authority are replaced by the acceptance of moral principles. Judgments of feeling are left behind.

Nor can we be beholden for our heredity. Whether character-traits are biologically transmitted is still a question for debate. In any case it would seem that if there is moral inheritance, it is an inheritance of behaviour tendencies rather than actual character-traits. Our moral responsibility would lie in the control of such tendencies rather than in the fact that we have inherited them. And the moral and spiritual environment here may be a determining factor.

*Sources of Behaviour*

We may come nearer to an answer to the question of *responsibility for* if we analyse the sources of behaviour.

Instinct is said to be a dying category in psychology. Nevertheless, we can with Lloyd Morgan speak of instinctive tendencies. Personally I like to think of the fundamental needs of the organism and of personality as evolving behaviour tendencies in the interest of satisfying these needs. The need for self-preservation is far more than an instinct of flight from danger; it involves the tendency to seek food when we are hungry, to sleep when we are tired and a host of other self-preserving tendencies. So the need for the procreation of our kind involves the need to love and be loved, the need not merely for sex satisfaction but for a companion; so the need for social status is far more than a herd instinct or a gregarious tendency; it may be the impulse behind our ambitions, of keeping up with the Joneses and it is the need for the respect of others. It is when our social status is threatened by unacceptable behaviour tendencies within us that we resort to unconscious repression and fall psychologically ill. It would not be untrue to say that psychological illness is an unconscious tendency to preserve our social status. Then we have the fundamental need for rational and moral unity. Intellect as contrasted with intelligence which we have in common with the animals, is the organ evolved in the interest of rational unity; conscience is the organ evolved in the interest of moral unity. We do not live comfortably either with an intellectual contradiction or a moral. Instinctive tendencies simply are; how we shall direct them or control them is due to cultural influences and our own insight. It is how we direct these tendencies that make us the subjects of blame or praise.

These needs and their correlated tendencies are motives; once they are active they tap the physical energy of the organism and thus move towards their ends. They solicit the Self but need not necessarily govern the Self.

### Motives, Habits, Sentiments, Complexes, as 'Symptoms of Readiness'

Gordon Allport rightly contends that behaviour and character involve what he calls *stable units*, which

'are always the product of the two central and vital functions of mental life: *motivation* and *organization*. It is regrettable that our psychological vocabulary inclines us to separate the two—the emotional forces from the cognitive or organizing force. From the point of view of actual conduct the primary unit of mental life is *organized motive*, or if you prefer *motivated organization*. Whatever it is called this unit is a *system of readiness,* a *mainspring* of conduct, preparing the person for adaptive behaviour whenever the appropriate stimulus or associations are presented.'[1]

There are different units; habits, e.g., are systems of readiness which 'are well-grained and fairly specific'. Thus all habits are acquired, e.g., capacity to drive a car, biting nails, masturbation. William James went so far as to say that character was simply a system of well-formed organized habits. When we speak of a character-trait we are thinking of a unit which is not so specific. Allport instances 'politeness', 'aggressiveness'; but we can include the 'perfectionist', and if we think of Karen Horney's[2] list of neurotic character-trends we get the disposition to seek approval and to fear disapproval, the seeking for prestige, etc.

On the other hand, we reach the most important structural unit so far as moral character is concerned in the very stable motivated organization named the *Sentiment.* Here we have a motivated organization of feeling, thought and conation directed towards an end, and organized round the idea of some object. We speak of a patriotic sentiment, a religious sentiment, a moral sentiment, etc. We may develop abstract sentiments as, for example, round the idea of justice, racial equality, sentiment for truth. There is no end to the sentiments we can acquire.

What are called 'interests' are a sort of quasi-sentiments as, for example, interest in football, in music, in art, in spastic children. The range of interests can be very wide and not a few of them can be very deep.

Sentiments may be negative or positive. McDougall said there were only two kinds of sentiments—those of hate and love. Structurally they are the same; but whereas the positive sentiment has for its end the good of the object, the negative sentiment has for its end the hurt or even the destruction of the object.

All these are normal sources of behaviour except the neurotic trends; these naturally lead to abnormal behaviour,

[1] *The Individual and his Religion,* p. 61.
[2] Cf. Karen Horney, *Self-Analysis.*

but not necessarily pathological. The motives of neurotic trends are as a rule rationalized.

One source of behaviour is very important; it is what Jung called a 'complex'. It is a system of readiness dissociated from the integrated part of the personality. It is repressed but manifests itself in consciousness, sometimes in serious abnormal behaviour as, for example, in compulsions. phobias, fear of contaminating people, exhibitionism, kleptomania. These complexes war against the normal personality. They are the source of our besetting weaknesses, or besetting sins and temptations, the elaborate ritual performances of some neurotics, and the simple but harmless ones of trying every switch to see that it is off or trying every door to see it is locked. Some people are compelled to bow to every church they pass, to remove everything elongated, such as pencils, before going to bed. In such behaviour we are perfectly aware of what we are doing but do not know why we should want to do these things.

So far I have not indicated the place of intelligence in behaviour. Naturally our intellectual processes by which we make comparisons, draw conclusions, anticipate consequences are important factors in guiding or criticizing our behaviour. Through intelligence we can become aware of how far our behaviour is relevant to the end we have in view. By utilizing past experience we are enabled to meet new and novel situations. In virtue of its capacity to grasp relationships it can relate our actual behaviour to what it ought to be.

It has been questioned whether either intelligence or intellectual processes can set us our ends. Thought, as Aristotle said, moves nothing. To McDougall instincts set our ends; here he largely followed Hume. Reason, however, is not to be identified with its organs. Intellectual process is a servant not a master. Reason is not to be identified with thought. It is the intellect that 'universalizes and formulates the material furnished by appetition in the same way as it universalizes and formulates the material furnished by sense perception'.[1]

[1] Burnett, *Ethics of Aristotle*, quoted by Laird, *Study in Moral Theory*, p. 124, *The Rational Good*, p. 64.

Both intelligence and the intellectual processes are servants of Reason. Reason itself is rooted in the fundamental need of personality for rational and moral unity. Reasoning and Reason must not be confused. If we cannot live comfortably with a moral or intellectual contradiction it is because the conative endeavour towards rational integration is inhibited. Reasoning is the process whereby we attempt to give grounds or to find grounds for such integration, but Reason itself is the impulse towards rational and moral interconnections, towards an organized whole of our experience. Reason is a function of the Self. Just as Will is the conative endeavour of the Self towards a particular end, so Reason is the conative endeavour towards a 'harmony of experience with feeling'. It is not, as Graham Walls reminded us, a subordinate activity on the order of the instincts, but a natural principle of co-ordination. It is General Smuts's 'Holistic principle' making for the whole we call personality. As Hobhouse put it in his *The Rational Good*:

'Reason is an organic principle in thought and so far as incomplete but progressive may be termed an organic impulse. So far as reality is finally intelligible to reason it must similarly be interpreted as an organic whole, so that we speak of Reason as the ultimate organic principle alike in thought and reality. Finally the fact that Reason, even as incomplete impulse, is the endeavour towards the whole which interconnects the parts is the basis of its sovereignty over every partial impulse or isolated belief, whatever degree of subjective certitude such belief may claim.'[1]

Certainly we have organic needs and biological ends which set some of our ends and intelligence is set the task of finding the means for their fulfilment. But there are personality needs which no biological urge can account for. The search for truth, both philosophically and theologically, the striving for justice and virtue, the obligation to fulfil our duty, these are ends set by the Reason. On the moral side conscience is the organ of Reason and is not to be identified with the negative Super-ego. The mature conscience says 'This is the way, walk ye in it'.                                    [1] p. 64.

I think it is well here to differentiate between motive and intention. They are not synonymous. Motive is not just a power that moves us. John Macmurray writes: 'The wind is the motive force which drives a sailing boat.'[1] Certainly the wind provides the sailing boat with power, but it does not 'sail' the boat, no more than 'the engine *drives* the car'. These misleading metaphors the Professor corrects on the following page. The engine and the wind have no explicit end. For a boat to be 'sailed' or a car to be 'driven' there must be some intended end. A human motive whether conscious or unconscious, as Drever defines it: 'is an affective-conative factor which operates in determining the direction of an individual's behaviour towards an end or goal, consciously apprehended or unconsciously.'[2] Motives are dynamic structures. Many motives become latent, but they are still 'systems of readiness' to act when the necessary internal or external stimuli are present. When a motive is active it is simply energy moving towards a conscious or unconscious definite end. Repressed motives are not latent they are dynamic, and always pushing their way towards consciousness. Freud calls an unconscious motive a 'wish'.

Unfortunately 'wish' and 'desire' are often used synonymously like motive and intention. A motive may be unacceptable to the conscious mind and as we have seen may be unconscious. Desire, like intention, is conscious. Hobhouse defines desire as 'impulse directed towards an anticipated end'.[3] Intention involves desire; it is conscious; but we may be mistaken and even self-deceived about our intentions. Freud's *Psychopathology of Everyday Life* is full of examples of mistaken and rationalized intentions. As a rule desire has a clear consciousness of its end.

All these, then, are sources of behaviour. How far are we responsible for these sources, for instinctive tendencies, habits, sentiments, interests, neurotic trends, complexes? Instinctive tendencies like our fundamental needs are given, our intelligence and reason are given; they are all what Macmurray

[1] *The Boundaries of Science*, pp. 241 f.
[2] *A Psychological Dictionary.*
[3] *The Rational Good*, p. 44.

calls 'facts'. Where, then, does responsibility come in? It comes in on the assumption that instinctive tendencies, sentiments, moral habits can only solicit, they need not govern. We are responsible for the conscious acceptance of our sentiments and interests, and for correcting evil habits. In so far as we allow these to govern we are responsible. Apart from that we are responsible for the manner in which we satisfy these tendencies. A man is not responsible for his sexual, or other desires or other impulses, but he is responsible for the means he takes to satisfy them. Many habits are acquired before we knew the real meaning of 'good' or 'bad'. We are, however, for ever correcting the habits we deplore. Character-trends may have been acquired or occasioned by our early environment. For example, an unwanted child, deprived of the love which it needs, may acquire the neurotic need for affection; a child brought up in a puritanic home may develop a neurotic need for perfection; a child born with some organic inferiority or some abnormality may react to the sense of inferiority by repressing that and then developing a neurotic need for power, for prestige; an unresolved Oedipus complex may be the root of homosexuality; a man born with an undropped testicle may resort to prostitutes to prove his virility. They may not be responsible for their condition, but they may be responsible for the expression of that condition. A homosexual is not responsible for his condition. He simply finds at adolescence that the other sex has no attraction for him; but he is responsible for homosexual acts, just as a man with strong promiscuous tendencies is responsible for giving way to them. Complexes are autonomous in the sense that they manifest themselves in consciousness without any act of will; they are not necessarily autonomous in their expression.

All these motives and tendencies to behaviour are largely determined in childhood. Many psychologists stop there. They take no account of the fact that at the same time as these are being acquired the Super-ego and later the conscience is being developed; and these have strictly to do with the control of such tendencies. Again, as intelligence and the intellectual powers grow they become determinants in behaviour. We may live, as Hare pointed out, by moral principles freely chosen, and the sense of responsibility engendered by both Super-ego and conscience should lead to moral decisions. True morality begins when our moral principles are insightfully seen as obligatory. 'Morality', as Hare writes, 'regains its vigour when ordinary people have learnt afresh to decide for themselves what principles to live by and more especially which principles to teach their children.'[1] Not what we desire but what we *ought* to desire becomes paramount.

It is this awakening of the sense of moral responsibility, that is to say, the moral consciousness, with its sense of *ought* and obligation, and its capacity for decision that makes possible the correction of what we have acquired through the environment of our childhood. With the growth of self-awareness habit becomes 'my habit', sentiments, 'my sentiments'; we feel responsible for them. To have moral principles, to be aware of morality, even Super-ego morality, would seem to involve the duty to realize them in our moral life. To be motivated by the sense of duty is probably the strongest motive we can acquire, for it is the outcome of the conative endeavour of Reason. It is certainly one of the most necessary motives in a moral life. Duty involves acting according to moral principles, for these are the content of duty. It is this which gives validity to Professor H. D. Lewis's definition of guilt as 'the betrayal of what I take to be my duty by which my conduct becomes directly morally evil and blameworthy'. Naturally we may be mistaken as to what our duty is in a particular situation, and we may even be mistaken about the moral principles themselves. Not a little unrealistic guilt and morbid guilt-feelings have their roots in mistaken moral concepts. The sense of duty does not guarantee the validity of the moral principles we hold, but it is dynamic; it is a conative urge to fulfil our duty; to disobey or even to neglect our duty means that the conative endeavour has to be overcome. So far as motives are concerned it would seem that they take root unconsciously; some are innate, but most of them are acquired without conscious effort. When I say 'I must

[1] *The Language of Morals*, p. 73.

learn to be more considerate', the motive to be more considerate is already incipient, and I can then cultivate the motive. We are responsible for cultivating our motives, and indeed for repudiating motives which the conscience condemns. Actually it is sentiments we cultivate, for virtues are qualities of our sentiments.

Motives, as we have seen, are dynamic structures, 'systems of readiness' to act; they have a conative 'tendency towards some end'. Once we know the end towards which they are soliciting us they can come under our control, unless they have become pathological, as in kleptomania. What is unconscious is not the tendency to steal, but *why we should wish to steal.*

It would seem, then, that it is our intentions for which we are responsible. I am responsible for my motives just in so far as their ends have become my intention. Motives and intentions can conflict and indeed do conflict in every temptation. In temptation I 'wish' something I do not desire, and indeed do not intend. John Macmurray gives the illustration:

'A man may be so angry that he is unable to control himself. He may find that against his conscious intention his anger determines his behaviour. In such cases the action has a motive in consciousness, and yet is not the realization of an intention of the agent. The distinction between motive and intention is clear in such an example. It is complicated, however, by the fact that the person may be mistaken about his motives in the true sense of the term. He may be under the influence of anger or jealousy without knowing it. Here we come upon one of the most distressing ambiguities in the meaning of the term "conscious". We are apt to say that such a person is jealous without being conscious of it. This does not mean that he does not feel the emotion that we call jealousy. If we include feeling in the meaning of the term "consciousness" then jealousy is in consciousness. He certainly feels it. On the other hand, he does not recognize it, and may be quite sure that he is feeling righteous indignation.'[1]

It has been contended that we cannot control our motives.

[1] *The Boundaries of Science*, p. 255.

It depends just what this means. If it means that we cannot help what comes into our conscious mind, it is true. But if it means that we cannot control the solicitations of what comes into our conscious mind it is false. The whole aim of psychoanalysis or psychotherapy is to bring the unconscious under the control of the conscious. In technical terms, to quote Dr Nunberg:

'The task of therapy, generally speaking, is to mobilize the energies of the id, to make the Super-ego more tolerant, and to help the ego regain its synthetic and sublimating faculties, as well as its own function of indisturbed perception and purposeful action.'[1]

If we put that into ethical terms then it means simply bringing all our systems of readiness to act under rational control, i.e. under the control of moral principles. In other words, it is our intentions, the ends towards which we are directing our emotions, conative tendencies and ideas that give moral value to our behaviour. Intentions are purely subjective phenomena. The *intending* is a subjective fact; but intentions mean that we 'intend a change in the objective world' or in our dispositions, and this future change is the intention of our actions. Naturally the intention must be linked with some motive if it is to receive the necessary energy to change the objective situation. To change an objective situation may involve changing my own motives and sentiments. Take a person dominated by a neurotic tendency to perfection. He is never satisfied with his achievements; he is compelled to find faults in himself. Such a person is dominated by the fear of vice rather than a desire for virtue; he spends his life *trying not to be bad* rather than directing his energies towards the good. For that person to become truly moral his whole attitude to morality has to be changed; the Self has to be changed.

## Character and the Self

That brings us nearer to what can be predicted as 'moral evil'. Long ago James Ward pointed out that character can

[1] *Psycho-analysis Today*, p. 57.

be predicated only of a Self. It is the Self that is guilty; it is the Self that must experience the guilt-feelings. 'Mea Culpa' said Augustine. 'How could I have done it?' cried a patient who had played with temptation until he fell. 'I feel defective in character' said another. If character can be predicated only of the Self then there must be close links between the Self and its character. 'Character is the larger and grander bearer of moral goodness' wrote Sir David Ross; but it is also the bearer of moral evil, in so far as character is the expression of the Self.

Character we may define as the synthesis of our moral and immoral principles which give direction to our moral lives. A weak character is one where the synthesis is weak; a bad character is one where immoral principles characterize the synthesis; a man of no character is one where there is little or no synthesis; the 'systems of readiness' are under no central control and are responded to without reflection or criticism.

We may, however, act out of character. We may often be overcome by habits difficult to alter, by complexes not integrated in the moral synthesis. The Self may be coerced by these non-integrated structures. It is on this that law bases its degree of responsibility. My impulses and 'systems of readiness' are mine but not 'me'. 'I hate the sins that made Thee mourn' wrote Cowper. 'That which I would not do, that I do, and that which I would do I do not', said the Apostle Paul. We can act out of character. The individual, nevertheless, does not excuse himself; he accepts his guilt-feelings.

We may also see a deterioration of character. The very personality may change. This can be due to a variety of circumstances. Disappointment in love, changed material circumstances, the return to adolescent habits and pleasures which had been left behind. Unlike a complex, character never becomes autonomous. 'There is no holiday in the moral life', I remember my philosophy professor once saying. Did not Sir John Seeley say 'No virtue is safe that is not enthusiastic'? The Christian Gospeller warns against backsliding. Jung contended even conversion does not obliterate old tendencies to behaviour.

To attempt to assess the degree of guilt here is beyond my

purpose, and indeed I think it would be a very difficult thing to do. Guilt-feelings are undoubtedly experienced and can be extremely intense, especially in old people. Often tendencies to which guilt was attached in childhood and which were repressed tend to press into consciousness in old people; only the guilt-feelings get in, although, in some, a phantasy element may enter and intensify the guilt-feelings. In some others the phantasy may express itself in action, then there is tragedy, the tragedy of some old respected member of the community in front of a court of law.

It is here I think Jung has something constructive to say when he calls for the admittance into the synthesis of character of the Shadow side of our personality. When it is integrated with our moral principles it is then under the control of character; and it has not much chance to act autonomously. People sometimes criticize religious hymns because they express contrition, or confession. 'My sins are ever before me' chants the Psalmist; 'False and full of guilt I am' repeats a favourite evangelical hymn. There is nothing morbid here; it is the acknowledgment of the Shadow side of our personalities. To be able to tolerate guilt-feelings without fear is, as Dr Winnicott said, the mark of moral strength not of weakness nor of morbidity.

## True Ethical Guilt Referred to the Self

True ethical guilt then seems to refer to a Self from which the evil has proceeded, and also to an objective situation. Reason, like sensation, and unlike emotion or intuition, is an objective function of the mind. As conscience is the organ of the reason, it refers to an objective situation, a moral order as the very nature of things. Ought and ought-not are imperatives, they are not options; virtuous living is living according to the moral nature of reality, and indeed with the Stoics I would say, 'according to reason'. The content of the ought may vary with cultural conditions and so may the concept of virtue. After all, our knowledge of the external world was not built up in a day; why should we expect that our knowledge of the moral order should be a less prolonged and laborious process? Character is not inherited nor is it given; our moral heritage unlike our intellectual and social heritage has to be re-experienced, re-lived by every generation. The growth of character and personality is in proportion to the degree we discover the moral order for ourselves.

Though the content of the ought is not given, the conative endeavour of the ought is present in every stage of organized life. In the primitive peoples the sense of ought is not less strong than in civilized man. It is a Super-ego ought; tribal law must be obeyed and guilt-feelings can be intense among them. But the push of a moral conscience must have been incipient from the beginning, otherwise moral progress could never have begun.

To the degree we become moralized, to that degree the positive conscience takes the place of the Super-ego; we grow beyond 'borrowed morality'. Nevertheless we never outgrow the Super-ego. Instead, however, of simply attempting to repress unacceptable impulses or emotions, or threatening us with punishment and guilt-feelings, its function in a mature conscience is to make us stop and consider what we are about to do. In the best of lives it is still capable of generating intense guilt when the conscience is disobeyed.

Before we close this section my attention has been drawn to Professor Braithwaite's 'Eddington Memorial Lecture'. If I understand him aright from Professor A. C. Campbell's Gifford Lectures, then he contends that when I say 'I ought to do X' what is primary in his 'pro-attitude' towards X is 'his intention to perform the action' when the occasion arises. One does not find this. I believe that such a pro-attitude involves an incipient resolve, or intention to do X. 'I ought to do X' solicits but does not govern. To resolve or intend the doing of X is a different moment in the moral experience. The conation of the conscience is towards the doing of X and makes the resolution easier to make, but does not contain the resolution. Conscience speaks with authority but it can be flouted, and the flouting can bring guilt-feelings or psychosomatic complications. One cannot flout the conscience with impunity.

## Freedom of the Self

From our discussion so far, it would seem that guilt is an ethical phenomenon for which we feel responsible and culpable. Linguistic analysis has become divorced from moral experience. We can see that in Professor Ayer's illustration of stealing. In moral experience 'stealing' is felt and judged to be wrong. Rightly or wrongly it is believed—granted that there is no pathological compulsion to steal—even by the person who stole that it was not necessitated, that he could have done otherwise, no matter what his previous character was. On that assumption our legal system rests, and without that assumption it is difficult to see how ethical science or philosophy could have meaning, to say nothing of the elaborate theological doctrines relating to sin and its forgiveness. I would go further and hazard the opinion that even psychoanalysis and all forms of psychotherapy rest on the fact that even if it were granted that we could not have done otherwise than we did *we need not do it tomorrow*. To blame ourselves is tacitly to admit that we think we could have acted otherwise; and to blame ourselves is not merely to be humiliated by other people's disapproval, but to experience the guilt-feelings which refer to the violation of some objective law. Even when it is granted that our character being what it is determined our act we still blame ourselves for our character. Character or no character, few people who have done wrong and suffer guilt-feelings are ready to admit that they could not have done otherwise. Even the alcoholic who has lost the power to control his drinking is loth to admit that he could not have resisted going into the public house yesterday and getting drunk. As Laird puts it: 'There is no obligation to pursue a good unless we can see this good (at least when it is pointed out to us) and unless the pursuit is psychologically possible, at any rate to the best of our belief.' It follows that there is no responsibility if I did not know it was wrong, or was psychologically unable to refrain from doing it. I find it hard to believe that I could not have resisted that extra smoke which accentuated my bronchitis!

So much has been written on the freedom of the Will that

H          113

one hesitates to add anything more. But the problem is fundamentally a psychological one. If we could not have done otherwise than we did, it is difficult to see how we could apportion praise or blame.

Naturally, psychology, like every other science is deterministic. To explain behaviour it has to look for and to describe causes. Whatever we may think of some of the concepts of psychoanalysis we must admit that it has laid bare the causes of much abnormal behaviour, either of feelings or acts. And no one will deny that the general psychology of character has added to our knowledge of how character and behaviour are related to definite motives, habits, sentiments and interests.

Psychological determinism, as we saw in the chapter on legal guilt, involves no more than the fact that human behaviour like all other kinds of behaviour, must have some cause. It does not follow from that that we could not have acted otherwise, indeed psychotherapy has for its very task the eliciting of some inner factor whose influence will help us to respond differently in the same circumstances. I doubt very much that psychological determinism involves that we always act on the strongest desire. There is no reason why self-determination should not be admitted as a causal agency. Do I need to give any other reason for my choice than simply that I think it is the best line to follow? After all, habits, interests, sentiments, are partial impulses whereas the Self acts in the interests of the personality as a whole. *That it does not do so is what has to be explained.* If Reason is the conative endeavour towards wholeness, towards 'harmony of experience with feeling', towards the 'prospective aim of personality', towards rational and moral unity, then it would seem to follow that the Self is free, and what has to be explained are the hindrances to self-determination. McDougall spoke of the Self-regarding sentiment as being the main element in character. But the Self-regarding sentiment is organized round the idea of the Self, whereas in self-determination it is 'the fact of the Self rather than the idea of the Self that is operative, although, to be sure, we may be

consistently supposed to have an obscure or virtual acquaint-
ance with this fact'.[1]

The Self is by no means to be identified with our character.
Character is the synthesis of all our 'systems of readiness', or
sources of behaviour. The synthesis may be weak because
the Self is weak, and there may be dissociated impulses and
complexes which are not modified by character, and tend to
act autonomously.

The Self is not born free. Freedom is an achievement;
freedom means, not the capacity for self-control, which is
always exhausting, as Bertrand Russell says somewhere, but
Self-possession. That means that I am in control of all my
sources of behaviour, my impulses, my sentiments, even my
complexes when they manifest themselves in consciousness.
Freedom means that I am not pushed around by my behaviour impulses. My impulses are *mine* but they are not *me*.
As we have seen the great majority of our sources of behaviour were acquired unconsciously and before I knew their
meaning as contrasted with their significance. I know they
had significance for they gave me pleasure. But once I know
their meaning morally, that they can generate desires which are
not desirable, I become responsible for them, and to the degree
that I learn to control them, or even eradicate them, to that
degree I become free, and Self-possessed. Self-determination is
substituted for impulse, habit or sentiment determination.

## Self-possession as Aim of Moral Education

Self-determination, Self-Possession, surely that is the aim
of all moral education, and indeed of cultural education.
Unless we are dealing with a moral genius like Christ, we
must not expect Self-determination or Self-possession to be
absolute. Only He has been able to say—and that at the end of
His life—'The Prince of this world cometh and findeth nothing
in me'. He had acquired perfect freedom. We can be tempted
only if there is something in us that can respond to the temptation. Few readers of this book need to run past a public
house lest they go in and get drunk. So, too, we need not keep

[1] Laird, *A Study in Moral Theory*, p. 141.

our hands in our pockets when going through an open market lest we steal some of the fruit. Really to be free is far more than a matter of being able to choose freely between open choices, between good and evil. To the degree we are morally free the evil will have lost its power to attract us. To the extent we are able to resist an undesirable desire to that degree we are not morally enslaved; but we cannot say we are free; we can still be tempted. Moral freedom in the true sense of the term is the fundamental aim of the moral life. A Self is free when it is able to pursue its self-imposed ends and inhibit tendencies which would oppose and hinder these ends. Self-control is not a virtue, though it may and indeed is a necessity for most of us. Self-control means that I have to be watching some of my behaviour tendencies like a policeman.

I have been using the term Self and not Will to describe the activities of moral experience. That is because Will is not an entity separate from the Self; it is a function of the Self, as can be inferred when I say 'I will to do this'. I do not will a choice; choosing to do something and willing to do it are one and the same thing. There is always the danger of hypostatizing functions into faculties working in their own right. When Augustine said 'My will does not obey me', he seems to imply that the Will and the Self are opposed to each other. But this is not the case. The Self's purpose may be inhibited by its own tensions or by competing inclinations. I am not denying that for descriptive purposes there is justification for using the term Will as though it were a noun. But Will is the Self in activity, just as memory is the Self remembering. All determination is self-determination, and the psychology of moral action is simply the study of what influences the Self in its determinations. Anger can influence the Self to hit out; politeness is the disposition of the Self to act courteously. We call these 'systems of readiness' to act in specific ways, but they simply describe ways in which the Self is influenced in its determinations.

### Could the Self have Acted Otherwise?

That brings us to the crucial problem as to whether the Self could have acted otherwise than it did. Yesterday, let us suppose, I got angry with my wife, and said hard, unkindly words which today I regret and indeed feel guilty and ask her forgiveness. If I am one of those men who have never cultivated the control of the expression of angry emotions, it is very doubtful whether I could have acted otherwise. Does that relieve me of responsibility and blameworthiness? Not a bit. I am responsible for the hurt and pain I caused, and for the fact that I have never cultivated control of my emotions. That is objective guilt.

Perhaps it is here that we see how freedom is acquired or even wherein we are free. My freedom may lie in learning from my experience. I may determine after realizing the evil of my behaviour yesterday that I ought to cultivate control of my emotions and learn to be 'angry and sin not'. I may have been unable to act otherwise than I did, but I can determine to act differently in future. In other words my emotions may become 'causes which do not necessitate' evil actions.[1] They can incline but do not necessarily determine.

On the other hand, if my self-regarding sentiment has a strong element of self respect and a firm idea of my duty to my wife, there is no reason why, in spite of the strong influence of my emotions, I should not be able to summon enough moral effort to overcome the impulse to say the hurtful things. There is always a reason—a motive if you like—for my behaviour. As far as psychology is concerned, there is no such thing as a motiveless act, or behaviour for which no reason can be given. Granted that I am justified in being angry with my wife, and granted again that I have a strong desire to say hurtful things, my self-respect and my sense of duty may intervene successfully to inhibit the strong instinctive desire. This is a free act where reason, not impulse, is the deciding factor. The impulse has its root in character; reason is the conative drive for moral unity, and indeed is the source of healthy self-criticism. My sense of duty is not an isolated impulse like anger or sex, but an element of

[1] Cf. Laird, *A Study in Moral Theory*, chapter 8.

conscience which is Reason's organ making for moral wholeness. When Reason acts, it is the Self that acts, and acts for
the good of the personality as a whole. Hence, the Self can be
a causal agency, uninfluenced by what others think or feel
about my actions.

But what about what people designate as 'the Strongest
Desire'? There is a danger of thinking of desire and impulses
as though they were physical forces. What we mean by a
desire being the 'strongest' is that it offers a strong immediate
release of tension in contrast to the strong moral effort to
realize some ideal end. It is not really analogous to the force
a billiard player imparts to a cue, and which sends the ball
into the desired pocket. It inclines the Self, or better attracts
him as a lovely landscape or vase attracts our attention, or as
the smell of a tasty dish invites us to partake. Motives may
attract us by presenting ends which offer an immediate
pleasure, but they cannot unless they are pathological push
us as the cue pushes the ball. Even a pathological motive
does not push us; we give way to it. In this way the freedom
of choice is undermined.

Professor Campbell speaks of a 'decision whether or not
to rise to duty';[1] and he believes, rightly, I think, that in face
of conscious moral temptation we can 'rise to our duty'. But
the sense of duty is something that characterizes the Self and
is causal. The content of our duty, however, is dependent on
our knowledge of good and evil and that knowledge can be
faulty; or our knowledge of good and evil may be purely
intellectual and unassimilated by our conscience. In that case
it lies over against our personality without influencing its behaviour. As we say, it is in a logic tight compartment. Already
we have mentioned Freud's 'knowing and a knowing', and
Hadfield's 'recognition and realization'. The sense of duty has
to be emotionally experienced, otherwise it plays little or no
part in our choices. It is through the sense of duty that we are
able to transcend our character, and can thus act contrary to
what has misleadingly been called 'the strongest desire', that
desire being no more than the one offering a more immediate

[1] *On Selfhood and Godhood*, Lecture 8.

satisfaction than the sense of duty. The knowledge of good
and evil must be assimilated, i.e. linked with our sense of
moral responsibility, otherwise it does not become a causal
factor. As Laird puts it: 'No emotional disposition is properly
a matter of conscience unless it is subordinate to the knowledge of good and evil'; in other words the knowledge of good
and evil, which is the basic content of our sense of duty, when
really a matter of conscience aids us in rising to our duty. If
we are inclined to say that our sense of duty is part of our
character then we can say that the Self has allies within
our character which explains why we can rise to duty when
faced with some attractive temptation. But the fact that we
can speak of 'self-criticism' implies 'a transcendence over
character'. If libertarianism means that we can act without
a ground for acting, behaviour could not be subject to explanation. When I regret what I did yesterday it is because
my sense of duty is today free from the inhibiting influence
of my anger yesterday. If my sense of duty today had been
as active yesterday then I could and would have acted otherwise. Determined behaviour can be perfectly free, because the
determining cause has been freely chosen.

Professor Lewis, if I understand him aright, limits freedom
to choice between open alternatives; he seems to have little
room for what Laird called 'settled determinations'. For
example, he writes: 'A kindly disposition does not lose its
importance by being no longer regarded as the subject of
distinctively moral praise.' He concedes that 'It may in fact
indirectly reflect moral worth, since we have a duty to cultivate a good character'. But immediately he withdraws the
meed of praise by the curious conclusion, 'But in itself it must
be classed with non-moral values, and as such will lose
nothing of its real character'. This from the ethical point of
view, is an extraordinary conclusion. A 'kindly disposition'
is a settled determination and it may be a causal factor in
my choice of the good and a factor in 'overcoming evil with
good'. Is a settled determination of no moral worth? Is 'a
supremely saintly person' to be discounted by the libertarian
when we come to appraise moral worth? To limit a man's

moral worth to the occasions when he resists evil seems to me to misunderstand the meaning of freedom. The less subject to temptation a man is the more free he is. The free man is not to be identified with the self-controlled man, but the self-possessed man—the man who can canalize his behaviour tendencies along the line of his freely chosen ends. To the degree he can be tempted to that degree is he potentially evil. Without a settled disposition towards duty, a pro-attitude towards it, he could not meet Campbell's demand to rise to duty. No wonder Professor Lewis has to confess that 'there is something paradoxical in the libertarian's view of moral worth'.[1] Here is part of the paradox: 'If the libertarian is to be heard, let it be on the claim that there is an unambiguous "open possibility", and that some of our actions at least could have been other than they are although everything else in the universe was the same.' If 'everything in the universe was the same' includes the individual who acted or made the choice, it is difficult to see how he could have chosen other than he did. He could have acted differently if some moral principle entered his conscious mind, which apparently didn't when he made his choice.

It is worth remembering that the opposite of 'free' is not caused, but 'compelled'. As Mrs Warnock has pointed out: 'The supposed inconsistency between freedom of choice and universal causation is shown to be non-existent since "freely chosen" and "caused" do not rule one another out'. The Self can choose its causes of behaviour. A rigid determinism would make us all compulsive neurotics; but a loose libertarianism would make choices arbitrary, capricious, motiveless and causeless. So far as psychology is concerned it knows nothing about either motiveless or causeless behaviour.

Ethical guilt, then, includes far more than 'some betrayal of what I take to be my duty'. I may have guilty emotions such as malice; I may have evil sentiments, evil dispositions, evil motives. To the degree that I allow such to govern me to that extent I am guilty and evil. In a word, just as good can be predicated only of a Self so evil can be predicated only

[1] *Ethics Since 1900*, p. 144.

of a Self because it has identified itself with its evil 'systems
of readiness'.

SELECTED BOOKS

*Morals and Revelation.* H. D. Lewis, London, George Allen &
Unwin.

*Language, Truth and Logic.* A. J. Ayer, London, Gollancz.

*The Language of Morals.* R. M. Hare, Oxford University Press.

*Ethics Since 1900.* Mary Warnock, Home University Library.

*Ethics and Language.* C. L. Stevenson, Yale University Press.

*Second Thoughts in Moral Philosophy.* A. C. Ewing, London,
Routledge & Kegan Paul.

*Ethics.* P. H. Nowell-Smith, London, Pelican Books.

*On Selfhood and Godhood.* C. A. Campbell, London, George
Allen & Unwin.

*The Freedom of the Will.* Austin Farrar, London, A. & C. Black.

# CHAPTER 5

# RELIGION AND GUILT

*Resumé*

WE have now seen something of the origin of guilt-feelings
and how they stem from the ambivalent tendencies towards
the mother's breast, and then towards the mother herself.
Anxiety begins in the infant in the fear of losing the loved
object through its own aggressiveness. With the birth of the
Super-ego, the anxiety acquires a special quality which turns
it into guilt-feelings. The Super-ego can make the child feel
that it is bad. The beginning of a neurosis or a psychosis may
have its ultimate roots here. The late Dr Ian Suttie[1] saw in
this sense of badness in the child the very seeds of melancholia.
With the dawn of an accepted sense of moral responsibility
for its behaviour, and its capacity to associate guilt-feelings
with actual behaviour we come to the birth of the positive
conscience in which guilt-feelings cease to be a moment in the
downward thrust of repression and become that moment of
contrition which is always a step upward in the development
of moral character and personality. It is in this experience
that the child catches a real glimpse of its capacity for freedom to choose between good and evil; it ceases to be a mere
acceptor of authority; and accepts the authority of the moral
principles taught by parents and teachers. To the degree the
child assimilates the moral principles it will comply with
them spontaneously. Later, however, as the growing adolescent gains moral insight, he will come to accept the principles
on rational or intuitional grounds. He, now, to use Hare's
language, makes his own moral decisions, and the principles
cease to be an imposed external law and become moral guides.
Whereas under the threats of the Super-ego he was compelled
to say 'I must' he now says 'I ought'. To the degree he falls

[1] *Origins of Love and Hate.*

short of obedience to his principles he experiences not merely subjective guilt-feelings but objective guilt; in other words his guilt-feelings are referred rightly to his objective behaviour. He experiences not the fear and threats of the Superego but true contrition.

Legal guilt we found was wholly objective. It was culpable and punishment was meted out. To what degree we are responsible for the legal guilt we have acquired is still an unsettled problem; and apart from the much criticized McNaghten Rules we are still without an agreed criterion of responsible and culpable behaviour. Psychiatrists and lawyers are still at war.

Ethical philosophers we saw, from Professor Lewis's *Morals and Revelation*, seem to shirk the term guilt. There are fundamental differences among ethical philosophers as to what their subject matter really is. To Hare, Ethics is the 'logical study of the language of Morals'; to Laird it is 'the Justification of imperatives'; to Hume, what is approved or disapproved by others, We must not forget, however, that Hume contended that what we approve or disapprove is not particular actions, but *character*, and the motives that go to make up character. To Ayer ethical statements are meaningless; they have an emotive value in the sense that they can stimulate moral behaviour, but they have no logical meaning. It has been said that 'the culprits who deny the psychological world can be studied in its own right and its own language' are 'aided and abetted by philosophers whom Sir Russell Brain has described as making a living by expounding the non-existence of their own minds'.[1] So it would seem that some ethical philosophers make a living by expounding the non-existence of ethical science. Apart from these differences about the subject matter of ethics there are great differences of opinion on the meaning of responsibility and freedom.

## Religion, Theology and Guilt

There are no differences of opinion, however, about the objectivity of guilt when we come to religion and theology.

[1] *Humanistic Psychology*, John Cohen, p. 24.

There are great differences as to the meaning of sin and its source. Some would root sin in the will of man, following Kant; others look upon sin as a necessity, following Hegel; still others seek to explain sin on empirical grounds, e.g. Tennant; but none would deny the reality of guilt nor its importance for the central tenets of the Christian religion. For the late Dr Orchard 'The Doctrine of Sin occupies an important and determinative position in the system of Christian theology. It diagnoses the disease and defines the injury that leave man in need of the Christian Redemption.' Father White goes further: 'Indeed', he writes, 'it may be said that without such a sense (of guilt) Christian faith and practice, the whole Gospel and message of Salvation, and the rites of the Church would be completely meaningless.'

We are not concerned here with the theological controversies about sin except in so far as they are related to the problem of guilt and the dissipation of guilt-feelings. That will raise problems enough! But we can say this, however: there is nothing more relevant to this anxiety and guilt-ridden age than what religion has to say about guilt and redemption.

## Does Christianity Stimulate Unhealthy Guilt-feelings?

Unlike either Law or Ethics theology takes cognizance of both subjective guilt-feelings and objective guilt. Whereas the task of the psychotherapist is to reduce the intolerance of the Super-ego, that is the intensity of guilt-feelings, the more evangelical theologians and preachers aim to produce the 'conviction of sin' by stimulating guilt-feelings. Jung thought Christianity had tended to increase and intensify these feelings. Others, however, such at Pfister, the Swiss Pastor, and one of the first to see the value of psychoanalysis for Pastoral Counselling, along with other psychoanalysts contend that Christianity has reduced guilt-feelings. Jung, nevertheless, gave great credit to the Church for providing symbols such as Atonement, Baptism, the Roman doctrine of the Sacrament of Repentance and the Confessional—reconciling sym-

Modern Theories of Sin, p. 1.
[2] Christian Essays in Psychiatry, p. 161.

bols he calls them—in virtue of which the guilt-feelings are dissipated and guilt-tensions reduced.

The general attitude of psychotherapists is rather against the stimulation of guilt-feelings, lest these feelings provoke morbid, inhibiting and joy-killing, misery, and indeed create neuroses. It is astonishing the number of patients they see whose neurosis is traced to something heard in preaching, or something read in supposed devotional books. Dr Guirdham in his *Christ and Freud* is emphatic that a good deal of the morbid guilt which comes to the consulting room is due to sheer 'clericalism'. 'Why should Christianity', he asks, 'be based to the degree it is on a sense of guilt? What, if anything, is there in common between a beautiful faith which has enriched culture and the crudities of tribal religion? Do we exaggerate the element of guilt in Christianity? I don't think so. . . . The litany begins with the phrase, "O God, the Father of Heaven have mercy upon us miserable sinners". In the Dissenting Churches there is less insistence on the verbal ritual of guilt and penitence, but the Non-conformist psychology reveals itself as riddled with guilt which expresses itself in clerical terms. It is not for nothing that we refer to the "Non-conformist conscience".'

He is especially hard on the doctrine of Original Sin, not only because of its lack of reasonable grounds, but because 'It does not allow for the fact that so many of us deliberately choose sin'.[1]

He is on more debatable ground, however, when he attributes the origin of the doctrine to 'ecclesiastical manufacture'. It is just as reasonable to premise that the doctrine was an attempt to account for the universality of sin rather than an ecclesiastical burden imposed on the soul of man.

It must not be thought that Dr Guirdham and those psychotherapists who think like him have any intention of belittling or explaining sin away. He goes so far as to write: 'It is reasonable that the individual should regard himself as unworthy in the eyes of God. We might almost say that this is an essential attribute of true religion and certainly

[1] *Christ and Freud*, Part Three.

few Christians would question such a view.'[1] What he detests, for like every psychiatrist he has to deal with it in his consulting room, is the 'self-paralysing attitude towards our own sin' stimulated by certain types of preachers, and the tendency to number amongst sins perfectly simple and innocent activities. In his volume *A Theory of Disease* he has little difficulty in showing that the narrower sects with their suspicion of even the simplest of pleasures, are more subject to psychosomatic disease and mental illness, especially obsessional states.

*Illustration of Co-operation Between Medicine and Religion*

Nevertheless, an over-powering sense of actual sinfulness can be a potent factor in depression, and can take away the will to get better of physical disease. As we shall see later, psychiatrists, especially in America, and to a small extent in Britain, are realizing that they have no psychiatric technique whereby they can dissipate real guilt-feelings. One illustration must suffice. I take it from an excellent small volume entitled *Spiritual Therapy*[2] by two ministers who are members of 'A Healing Team' consisting of physician, surgeon, nurse, psychiatric worker and chaplains, in North Carolina Baptist Hospital. The citation of the case is made by the senior editor of the *Reader's Digest* in an Introductory Foreword. Briefly stated it was: A young mother was involved in a car crash in which her baby was killed. Though badly injured, she was skilfully treated by the surgeon; but she made little progress towards recovery. There being no medical reason why she should not recover, the surgeon called in the psychiatrist; the latter's analysis uncovered the reason for her failure to respond to treatment: the baby who was killed in the smash was the result of an extra-marital affair. She had kept her secret well. The guilt, however, which she had repressed or held in check, now came back on her; and now nothing the psychiatrist could say could shake the guilt-ridden interpretation of the accident's meaning for her. 'I've got to die', she kept on repeating. 'It's God's punishment for my sin.'

[1] *A Theory of Disease*, p. 41.
[2] *Spiritual Therapy* by Young and Meiburg.

The psychiatrist could get no further, so he called in the chaplain. The analysis could go no further than lay bare the trouble. The chaplain, one of the authors of the volume, visited the patient several times, allowing her to express her guilt, and then brought to bear upon the guilt the Christian doctrine of forgiveness, and truly Christian wisdom. 'Wouldn't you like', he asked, 'to use this tragedy to redeem your marriage?' That was what she did; the wounds healed rapidly; and she redeemed her marriage.

Here the guilt was real; the guilt-feelings referred to an objective situation. The self-punishment she morbidly demanded she projected upon God; for we cannot forgive ourselves.

There need be no antagonism between psychiatrist and minister. The priest or minister does not need to create guilt-feelings; they are there in us all though often hidden or disguised. Every psychotherapist knows that the symptoms brought to him often stem, like the young mother's, from real guilt which has been repressed. However we interpret the experience of it, that experience is widespread in the modern world as can easily be inferred from the novels and the poetry of Eliot and Auden. But it is overwhelmingly felt as, e.g. Quentin in Faulkner's story, *The Sound and the Fury*, and it finally drove him to suicide. It may not be felt at all as in the central figure in Camus's *Outsider*.

## Divorce of Guilt from Redemption

Hidden or conscious, the sense of guilt has been very largely divorced from the religious doctrine of Redemption, as Lewis J. Sherrill has shown in his interesting volume *Guilt and Redemption*. By far the great majority of those afflicted with guilt-feelings, disguised often in psychosomatic disease or psycho-neuroses, go to the psychotherapist for relief from their suffering and misery. They are not concerned to be 'redeemed' from sin, but to get rid of the intense misery of their feelings.

What should be noted is that the gulf between the theologian's and the preacher's concept of guilt and sin and that of the common use of the term by ordinary people, novelists and the psychologist is wide and deep. Sin or guilt as used even in common conversation does not connote anything in man's relation to God, but rather an inner experience of emotional conflict which may or may not be referred to a breach or failure to reach some personal standard or cultural standard of morality. Seldom is such a breach felt as falling short of the glory of God.

To the theologian sin is equated with guilt. My old Professor of Systematic Theology began his lecture on Sin by saying: 'Gentlemen, sin is guilt.' Barth says the same thing in his commentary on Romans, the implication being that guilt is the relation in which man stands to God.

We have already seen that the analysis of ethical guilt implies that we are responsible for our morality; and that we are responsible both to society and ourselves. Both religious experience and theology have no difficulty in asserting our responsibility to God. 'Against Thee, Thee only have I sinned and done this evil thing' (Psalm 51). Indeed sin is a purely theological term and always has reference to our relationship to God, or to some contravention of what is regarded as divine law, or the Will of God. As there is none good but God (Luke xviii) we are all sinners guilty in God's sight: 'All have sinned and come short of the glory of God' (Romans iii).

## The Theological Meaning of Guilt

I am greatly indebted to Professor T. Torrance of New College, Edinburgh, one of our foremost theological scholars, for an excellent and lucid description of the theological meaning of objective guilt.

'Objective guilt', he writes, 'goes down to the roots of man's existence. His sin takes place within the life-relation which he derives from God. He uses the very life and being which God gives him and maintains in him—even when he sins—to sin against God, and so introduces a contradiction into his being and existence. It is at that level that God opposes him, even when God gives and still regards him as made for God and for communion with God. Hence, deep in man's existence we have this difficult state.

'On the one hand, he lives by deriving his being and life from God, and God continues to give Himself to man in spite of his sin. On the other hand, this Self-giving of God to the sinner is the active love of God that counters and opposes the movement of sin in man, his self-will. Hence the opposition to man's sinful motions, or God's judgment upon sin enters as a determining element in the existence of man as estranged from God. Guilt is thus rooted in man's existence, in the divine "No" to his sin-determined and selfishly orientated existence. This element of guilt is made acute by the pouring out of God's Love in Christ, for now God does not hold Himself back, but actively seeks the sinner for his salvation, and in that *lovement* the tension of guilt is brought to its most acute point and brought out into the open—hence the Cross.'

Now that is an excellent description of theological objective guilt. Redemption and guilt are linked together.

## Objective and Subjective Guilt

On subjective guilt-feelings Professor Torrance writes: 'This is man's feeling of guilt, or awareness of guilt. He cannot have this without real guilt; but as objective guilt it can be detached and become almost something in itself—e.g. as in Greek tragedy—which needs catharsis or purging somehow.'

He might have added that there is this tendency to detach sin so that it becomes something in itself in St Paul. We have the well-known passage in Romans chapter vii where St Paul speaking of the conflict with sin within himself writes: 'For that which I do I allow not: for what I would, that I do not, but what I hate that do I. If then I do that which I would not, I consent unto the law that it is good. Now then it is no more I that do it, but sin that dwelleth in "me".'

What is common to Professor Torrance and St Paul here is that sin is no mere absence of good, but a positive resistance to good; it is active resistance to God—a using of the life God gives and sustains to resist and even to rebel against

Him. It is not mere 'estrangement'—a favourite word of Tillich's—it is an active denial of man's essence, and 'introduces a contradiction into his being and existence'.

If I understand Dr Torrance aright, then the theology implicit in the written communication to me, is that of what is called 'The Confessional School of Theology'. It is a theology relevant to the on-going life of the Church. As one writer has put it: it moves 'in the realm of faith, that is, it seeks to confront us with that which it believes to be the truth which lays a claim upon us, namely the commitment of our whole Self. Such authority is of the utmost importance for the on-going life of the Church. It affirms, it asserts, proclaims. But it is a setting forth of beliefs; it is not knowledge, at least that is verifiable.'[1]

Confessional theology sees its task as an examination and proclamation of what is revealed in two ways. Now I use Dr Torrance's own words:

A. 'To set forth in general terms what is revealed about the human situation as it is seen by the eyes of the Father; and

B. In the light of that, and especially in the shadow of the Cross itself, to understand as far as we may, the enmity of man, and the meaning of sin. Then we can go forward to understand more fully and clearly the atoning death and justifying resurrection of Christ.'

Personally I am all at one with this school (which is really Barthian) in believing that God in Christ is burdened by our griefs, pains and sins; that He does not will the destruction of any, but on the contrary wills that man shall be made whole; and that God allies Himself against sin which introduces the contradiction into man's nature.

## Experience and Theology

But the one thing we cannot do today is to confront man simply with what is said to be revealed. After all the sources of theology are experience, the experience of God, the experience of Revelation, if you like. Its business is to clarify what

[1] *The Fear of God*, p. 100.

men have experienced of God, to interpret and systematize what experience has handed down. Our experience of God must be correlated with our experience of man. We need to know what there is in man whereby he is able to respond to God or whether there is anything that can respond. It must begin with the empirical fact that man is a sinner, not with the *a priori* concept of a 'Fall'. Guilt is an experience before it is a concept; redemption is a fact of experience before it is a theory of the Atonement. Revelation was an experience before there arose the theological doctrine of Revelation. 'I am the Lord thy God; thou shalt have no other Gods beside me' is a conviction rooted in the numinous experience of the writer, before he exalted it into the first commandment. It is the experience of great religious lives which is the inspiration of religion, not its dogmas. As Whitehead says: 'Religions commit suicide when they find their inspirations in their dogmas. The inspiration of religion lies in the history of religion. By this I mean that it is found in the primary expressions of the intuitions of the finest types of religious lives.'[1] The value of dogma lies in the fact that it tends to elicit the experience which the dogma formulates. Hence the dogmas of guilt and redemption must not be divorced from life as people know it. Otherwise people are estranged from religion rather than drawn to it. As Lewis Sherrill[2] wrote: 'they turn from the theologian's concept of sin as from something with which they have no concern. There is a worse reaction when they are confronted with enmity to God, or with their total depravity.' To the psychologist and indeed to the lawyer the totally depraved are known as psychopaths and little can be done with them.

Let us grant that there is revelation of man's sinfulness and guilt, and God's attitude to it, that revelation has to be interpreted. It cannot be received passively. Even when we say, as the Confessional School of theology would say, the revelation offered to us is not information but Christ Himself, Christ is already interpreted as Reveler of God and Saviour

[1] *Religion in the Making*, p. 129.
[2] *Guilt and Redemption*, p. 13.

from our guilt. It is what is said to be given in the revelation which is questioned. For any revelation to be 'saving knowledge' there must be an element of interpretation. It is not easy to accept as a Gospel something that is thrown at you with 'Take it or leave it'. It is no revelation until one has interpreted it. That interpretation is bound to be coloured by one's past experience, by the content of the religious sentiment already acquired in our upbringing and culture. 'Barth understands the Word in accordance with the particular traditions in which he was reared; and his understanding is at variance with other men who are, so far as we have any way of knowing, also Christian.'[1]

This would not, however, confute either Dr Torrance or Dr Barth. They can at once answer that theology is perfectly relevant *after* we have been *determined* by the Word of God; but it can only be used to explicate what is given; it cannot be based on experience, for experience can tell us nothing about God. Theology can illuminate what revelation gives, it cannot inform it. As Berthold truly says of Barth's position:

'There is no structure of human experience which even discloses the possibility of a relation to God. *The possibility of knowing God is created new in the moment in which God makes Himself known.*'[2]

It is beyond my purpose to enter into a lengthy discussion of the Barthian position, even if I were competent to do so. We are concerned only with the elucidation of the meaning and significance of guilt as the theologian expounds it. It is our contention that the analysis of the experience of guilt and religious anxiety—and guilt, remember, is anxiety with a special quality—can tell us something of man's relation to God; it tells us that we are separated from God, and yet that we desire Him. Psychologically it is the condition in which God's revelation can be experienced and interpreted. Barth's position is well summed up in these sentences from Professor Norman Robinson's *Christ and Conscience*: 'From the

[1] *Fear of God*, p. 124. The whole chapter should be read.
[2] *Fear of God*, p. 121.

character of man's anxieties we can learn nothing about God, either about whether He exists or how He is related to man. But from being transformed, illumined, determined by the Word of God, we can come to understand our anxieties. Thus the Word of God with its message, as Barth would insist, of total depravity must stand as the fixed point in all our reasoning about anxiety.'

## Total Depravity

No psychologist will deny the depths of depravity to which a human being can sink. Neither Freud nor St Paul's first chapter in the Epistle to the Romans goes too far in their descriptions of the sins human beings can commit. But it is a far cry from the catalogue of particular sins to the doctrine of the total corruption of human nature. If we grant that human nature is totally depraved then from the psychological point of view man would have nothing within himself with which he could respond to any moral or religious appeal; and the only way out would be the Barthian doctrine of an invasion of grace, or *creation out of nothing*. If Biblical scholars have questioned Barth's interpretation of the Biblical attitude to sin and salvation, and Richard Niebuhr and Berthold,[1] to mention only two, have done so, there can be no question of the psychologist's right to question his interpretation of human nature. And this he can do from the very experience of religious anxiety and guilt.

## Estrangement

That man is estranged from God (and that is really his religious predicament) the psychologist need not deny, if we mean by estrangement what Paul Tillich means, namely, that 'Man as he exists is not what he essentially is and ought to be'. That 'we have all sinned and come short of the glory of God' needs no proof. Whether this estrangement is first of all consequent on our creation, as Tillich holds, or due to what the theologians call the 'Fall', is scarcely a question for the psychologist. To Tillich creation involves 'the transition

[1] *Fear of God*, p. 125.

from essence to existence. (God) creates the newborn child, but if created it falls into a state of existential estrangement'.[1] This kind of estrangement is not sin. This experience of estrangement can arouse religious and philosophical anxiety but not guilt.

### Essence and Existence

We do not, however, lose our essence when we are brought into existence. Indeed, on the contrary, our ethical and religious *telos* is to realize that essence in existence. To say with Sartre that man has no essence would mean that he is the one living thing who has no *telos*, no directing end that gives meaning to his life. Ethical anxiety arises immediately we become acutely aware that we are not realizing our essence, that we are not as we ought to be. Existential anxiety arises not because we have no meaning, but because we have lost it; we are estranged from our meaning or essence. Existence precedes, not our essence, but the realization of it. To get rid of essence Sartre has to get rid of God. But the fact that he can speak of *Existentialism as Humanism* shows that in his mind he has some thought of what a man ought to be. Be that as it may, the fact that we experience estrangement, that we can experience existential anxiety would imply, as Tillich argues, that we are estranged from what we really are or were meant to be. 'Man', writes Tillich, 'is not a stranger to his true being, for he belongs to it. He is judged by it but cannot be completely separated, even if he is hostile to it. Man's hostility to God proves indisputably that he belongs to Him. Where there is the possibility of hate, there and there alone, is the possibility of love.'[2]

The sense of ethical estrangement is the awareness that we have failed and are failing to realize our true ethical being. It is not a matter of violating our sense of ought, or even the betrayal of our sense of obligation and responsibility. Rather it is the sense of resistance to the demands of our ethical being. We may not be immoral, but conscious of our resistance or reluctance to obey the ethical imperatives of our true being.

[1] Ibid, p. 50.
[2] *Systematic Theology*, vol. 2, p. 52.

## The Sense of Ought and Bondage

I think this is what Brunner should mean when he writes: 'Duty and genuine goodness are mutually exclusive. Obedience due to a sense of unwilling constraint is bondage.'[1] 'Bondage' is probably too strong a word. The fact that I obey in spite of an 'unwilling constraint' shows that however estranged I am from my true ethical being, I am aware of it, and indeed comply with it. My feeling of estrangement stems from my awareness of the 'unwilling constraint'. Thus I am not a stranger to my ethical essence.

Let us, however, confine ourselves to religious estrangement. Again what we find here is this resistance to God. I cannot bring myself to call it 'hostility to God'. No doubt there are people who really experience hostility to God, but it is always hostility to some concept of God rather than to God Himself. I have never found in the analysis of estrangement that an aggressive hostility is a necessary element. 'The sense of ought,' writes Brunner, 'shows me the Good at an infinite, impassible distance from my will. Willing obedience is never the fruit of the sense of ought, but only of love'.[2] Put in terms of existentialism, this simply means that willing obedience comes when I identify myself with my essence. What I *ought* to do has become what I *want* to do. Estrangement ceases when that has come to pass. Religiously that means that I have identified myself with God's will. Or as St Paul puts it: 'I live yet not I but Christ liveth in me' (1 Timothy v).

The anxiety arising from the sense of estrangement may be due to sin. As Tillich reminds us: 'Estrangement cannot replace sin.' It is not a synonym for sin. To quote again: 'The word "sin" cannot be overlooked. It expresses what is not implied in the term "estrangement", namely, the personal act of turning away from that to which one belongs. Sin expresses most sharply the personal character of estrangement over against its tragic side. It expresses personal freedom and guilt in contrast to tragic guilt and the universal destiny of estrangement.' 'Man's predicament is estrangement, but his

[1] *The Divine Imperative*, p. 74.
[2] Ibid, p. 74.

estrangement is sin.'[1] I would rather say has become 'sin'. The original estrangement is consequent on passing from essence to existence. There is no sin here. Nevertheless, it can be thought of as a 'Fall'. The babe in the womb is not a sinner. But once it is born it is potentially a 'sinner'.

## The Meaning of Sin

But what do we mean by this term 'sin' which is equated with guilt? It is the cause of personally created estrangement, or better still, of the sense of alienation from God experienced in the guilt-feelings. What actually is the nature of 'sin'? What is 'Original Sin' in the true sense of 'original'? I am not thinking of Adam's sin. So much ingenuity has been applied to the interpretation of the Biblical Myth, that I am leaving it alone. Nevertheless, there is real meaning to the term 'original sin'.

Theology is not lacking in definitions of sin. Even psychologists have taken a hand in the task of defining sin. Dr Hadfield, e.g., differentiates *moral disease* from sin in this way: 'Sin', he writes, 'is due to wrong sentiments, moral disease is due to morbid complexes giving rise to uncontrollable impulses. The full and efficient cause of sin is a deliberate and conscious choice of the will moved by a false or wrong ideal.' The late Professor H. R. Mackintosh spoke of 'Sin as essentially selfish'. In his *Human Nature in the Remaking* Hocking has a chapter on 'Sin as Blindness and Untruth'. Leonard Hodgson defines sin as 'conscious disobedience to God's will'. A great deal is made by various theologians of conscious 'disobedience' and 'rebellion', 'antagonism' to God. Mackintosh speaks of 'the wrong attitude of the will', and says that 'the distinctive quality in sin lies not chiefly in its antagonism to our higher life, or to the welfare of society, but in its antagonism to the will of the living God'. It is doubtful if even the repentant sinner would experience 'antagonism'; he acknowledges he has followed his own will, even preferred it to God's will, but active antagonism is more a neurotic symptom than the essence of sin.

[1] *Systematic Theology*, vol. 2, p. 51 f.

*Sin and Ego-centricity*

From the psychological point of view (and it need not contradict the theological view, indeed confirms the more classical definitions of sin) the root of all our sins is Ego-centricity. From its very birth the child is Ego-centric. Indeed the child's growth morally and spiritually can be measured by the degree it passes from Ego-centricity to Object-centricity. The extreme Ego-centred person consciously or unconsciously *makes himself his own main purpose.* Everything and everybody becomes grist to his mill. He may achieve great things in any sphere or sink to the level of the beast, but the motivation is the same in both cases. He may be 'holy' but the motivation may be self-display; he may take a pride in his 'holiness', or he may be dominated by a neurotic desire for approval and a fear of disapproval; he may win battles for his country and the motivation be his own Ego-centric will; he may be generous to charity with a show of sympathy, but again the motivation may be self-seeking. But why go hunting for illustrations? Have we not an excellent contrast between Ego-centricity and Object-centricity in St Paul's great chapter on love? 'Though I speak with the tongues of men and of angels and have not love, I am become as sounding brass or a tinkling cymbal. . . . And though I give all my goods to feed the poor, and though I give my body to be burned, and have not love, it profiteth me nothing.'

*Sin and Sins*

Ego-centricity which is sin and not a sin, pollutes the whole activity of the individual to such a degree that it becomes the principle of that person's character and personality. What is lust but the Ego-centric desire to use another for the gratification of one's own pleasure? Once the lust is satisfied there is the tendency to turn away from the object that gratified it. It is concupiscence in the true sense of that term. What is greed but the seeking of the things that others cannot share? What is Adler's Will to Power but the Ego-centric desire to get one's way by hook or by crook? People who break down because of this Ego-centred will rule the house from the sick bed. It is true to say that every neurosis can be interpreted in terms of protecting the Ego-centric self or of getting something that otherwise it could not get. Pride, envy, anger, covetousness, gluttony, lust, sloth, these deadly sins of Catholic theology can be explained without remainder by the principle of Ego-centricity. It corrupts everything it touches. Analyse the villains of classical drama or the novel and the principle is manifest. Analyse the villains of history and you find them explained by the same principle.

But it is the principle of Sin in every one of us. We are all tainted with its corrupting force. All sins stem from its corrupting root.

Tillich analyses estrangement as sin into Unbelief, Hubris and Concupiscence. These he says, are the marks of estrangement due to Sin. Are these not the marks of Ego-centricity? The one belief of the Ego-centric is belief in himself; he trusts nobody but himself; he is the object of his own faith. 'Hubris', writes Tillich, 'is the self-elevation of man into the sphere of the divine.' 'It is the "spiritual sin",' writes Tillich, 'and all other forms of sin have been derived from it, even sensual ones'. Hubris is a particular sin, not SIN. I doubt if it can be equated with Ego-centricity, but it is certainly one of the marks of it.

So with Concupiscence: it is bred and propagated by Ego-centricity.

## Object-centricity

We can see the evil of Ego-centricity if we contrast it with Object-centricity. The object-centred personality is motivated by the person or cause or activity in *whose services he has enlisted*. Instead of pressing everything into the service of himself, he is enlisted in the service of whatever has captured his interest. He is motivated by the good of the object. The centre of gravity of his personality is without, not within. We grow within but not from within; we grow from without.[1]

The most object-centred principle of personality is love,

[1] Cf. *Psychology and God*, by Grensted, whose whole argument is built on this premiss.

using that term in the wide sense. Love obliterates the gap between being governed by the 'ought' or the 'must' and willing constraint. We can go back to St Paul, and if we examine the constituents of love in his analysis, we find that every one of them is object-centred: 'Love seeketh not her own' (1 Cor. xiii). In love we are enlisted, not conscripted in the service of the loved object. 'For their sakes I sanctify Myself', said Jesus (John xvii). 'The glory which Thou hast given Me I have given them' (John xvii).

The mystics and spiritual directors of the Church named Ego-centricity 'Self-love'. Hence their *via negativa*—the attempt to eradicate the Ego-centricity of self-love. Ego-centricity is deeper than self-love. Fromm lays great emphasis on accepting self-love; and Christ gave as the second commandment loving our neighbour as ourselves. Self-hate is a neurotic symptom, not a virtue.

Sin, then, is Ego-centricity; and we are sinners to the degree in which our attitude is Ego-centric. To the degree we are motivated *for* the self we are Ego-centric. Selfishness is only one aspect of Ego-centricity. The Ego takes the place of God, it is a principle that dominates the personality and our whole make-up.

### Are We Wholly Evil?

Are we wholly evil or Ego-centric? The infant seems to be wholly Ego-centric. But Ego-centricity before the dawn of self-consciousness has no moral significance except for those whose duty it is to redirect the child's tendencies towards Object-centred activities. To the degree the parents elicit love for themselves and for others to that degree the child becomes Object-centred. The struggle for Object-centricity begins in earnest, the moment the growing child becomes aware that a prohibition is laid upon some forms of behaviour, and a 'must' or command on other forms. Moral development is from Ego-centricity to Object-centricity. The very fact that we have this potential capacity for moral development rules out the concept of total depravity. Totally corrupt we could not even begin to be moral.

Nevertheless, we must not try to go to the opposite extreme and take the capital letter from Sin, and simply talk about sins. After all, when we experience guilt-feelings, it is not for what we have done but for what we are. When we pray for forgiveness it is not simply that we think of particular sins we have committed and seek pardon for them: we seek forgiveness as selves. It is we who have to be forgiven, not our sins. We seek pardon for sins, forgiveness for ourselves. That is obvious when we remember that forgiveness is not merely a pardoning of sins, but a restoration of the interpersonal relationships which our sins disturbed. Our sins cannot be undone; the physical and psychological effects of these sins, it may be impossible to remove. But the soul may be restored, the burden of guilt lifted, and an end made to the estrangement and alienation.

I have approached the doctrine of religious guilt and the experience of guilt-feelings from the 'Human end'. That is probably because as a psychologist one sees the awful suffering and misery of guilt-feelings. These feelings can produce a horrific sense of alienation from one's self, from one's family and from God. I would not ignore Dr Torrance's reminder that Confessional Theology sets forth its proclamation of guilt in general terms as revealed and 'as seen by the Father'. Not only so, but Confessional Theology does link up guilt with life as lived. He is perfectly aware of unrealistic guilt, and like Professor H. D. Lewis he thinks that unrealistic guilt-feelings, whose roots are in the fear of consequences, gain their intensity from the fact that they hide the sin and the guilt before God. Professor Lewis writes: 'One wonders whether pseudo-guilt with its roots in fear and retaliation, would have quite the tone that it has were it not for its resemblance to genuine guilt.' Alongside that let me quote Dr Torrance:

'I look upon the feeling of guilt as the subjective counterpart to real guilt, but as something that can be pathologically detached, and exert its pain in odd places. Thus the feeling of guilt can behave like referred pain in the body. If I have a pain down my left arm and in my shoulder, it is no good doctoring the arm when it all comes from the heart. It is the heart trouble that needs dealing with. That is the problem with guilt—the deepest guilt—objective guilt is man's heart trouble, but the pain of it can be felt in all sorts of experiences, referred to different parts and attached to different acts and experiences where it does not properly belong. Then this subjective guilt can become objectified on its own, as it were, and needs to be dealt with as a powerful damaging force— that is the job of the psychologist or psychiatrist; but when he has dealt with that referred guilt, even in its self-objectifications, he still has not dealt with the deepest root of the problem which is sin and guilt before God, and which can be dealt with only by objective Atonement, by real forgiveness that undoes the sin and blots out the guilt; then the feelings of guilt have to be cleared up. Much of the feeling ought to clear up at once with radical forgiveness, but the pathological effects of guilt cannot always be cleared up easily, and then these have to be dealt with by people like you.'

Now, both these writers are right in emphasizing a relation between displaced guilt-feelings and guilt, and real objective guilt. I have already given illustrations of displaced guilt; and Dr Sherrill gives a whole chapter to 'The Outcropping of Guilt' with illustrations of how the unconscious can displace the guilt in its attempt to 'save face'. The guilt may express itself in psychosomatic symptoms as well as in 'referred' anxiety-feelings. I have given a striking illustration from the medical journal, *The Lancet* in my volume *Nervous Disorders and Religion* of the young doctor with tuberculosis whose positive response to treatment was held up by what his Church would call unconfessed 'mortal sin'. On the other hand we see many people whose guilt-feelings arise from wrong concepts of moral imperatives or religious demands. Brought up in a Scottish home where travelling by train on Sunday was considered as 'Breaking the Sabbath Day', I suffered severe guilt-feelings when as a student in England I had to travel to my preaching appointment on the Sunday. I felt I was a hypocrite, preaching and yet breaking the Sabbath. It was a horrible feeling, and it took me some time to realize that my feelings of guilt were purely subjective and morbid.

Not a little of adolescent guilt-feelings are due to a misunderstanding of sex impulses and feelings; and indeed many good Christian people never get rid of guilt-feelings in regard to sex. Ambivalent feelings towards parents can cause uneasy guilt-feelings in the adolescents unconsciously struggling for individuation. Undesired but compulsive phantasies is another cause of these unrealistic guilt-feelings. I would hesitate to agree with Dr Torrance that ultimately all guilt-feelings must be referred to objective guilt before God.

## Exploitation of God by Parents

A prolific source of these subjective guilt-feelings is the exploitation of God by parents who want a short cut to the discipline of their children. God is often used as a big stick to punish the children if they have done wrong, or to prevent naughtiness through fear of God. A good example comes from a recent edition of the *Scotsman*. In the 'Scotsman's Log' the writer told of a visit to the Western Highlands. While staying at one manse he accompanied the minister to the Church service. The small son of the minister took the opportunity of his father's absence to trample a bed of lovely flowers in the garden. They were favourite flowers of the minister, and very naturally he could not have been too pleased to see them trampled and useless. He said to his son: 'Were you not afraid God would see you trampling the poor flowers?' That is the kind of thing which becomes a part of the child's Super-ego, his negative conscience, and can add to the fear of the corporal punishment that might be inflicted, or the withdrawal of both the parent's love and God's love. Apart from that there is incorporated into the child's idea of God, the picture of God as a snooper. Fortunately, as the writer tells us, the child met the threat of God seeing him with the reply: 'Oh no. I knew that God was with you in the Church!' Nevertheless, the idea would stick. It is the simple germ of what grows into the concept that every sin has to be paid for, an idea still implicit in certain doctrines of the

Atonement, and in the Roman doctrine of penance. Father White puts it quite plainly: 'The acceptance of free and gracious forgiveness is not enough to relieve us of the sense of guilt: *it must be paid for*. (The italics are mine.) The need to atone for real or supposed guilt is endemic in human nature: the sacrifice of the Cross, which the Church re-presents daily in the celebration of the Eucharist meets a deep emotional need without which full atonement is impossible.' Yet Father White knows well the effect that 'faulty, one-sided or ill-timed religious teaching can be a real factor in obsessive guilt'. The idea that every sin has to be paid for is rooted in the Super-ego and not in the adult conscience. The whole idea makes the relation between God and man a judicial one. It is those people with the idea that our relation to God is judicial who are liable to scruples, or as Miss Petre, the Catholic modernist, called them 'spiritual vermin'. She knows for in her teen-age sin had become an obsession and the 'spiritual vermin' troubled her badly. Common in those people with the judicial idea of God are the disturbing neurotic character-trends, perfectionism and the restriction of their lives within narrow limits. Motivated by neurotic guilt they are continually finding flaws in themselves, and attaching guilt to perfectly innocent pleasures. One woman was so burdened by these neurotic character trends that she gave up religion, and said the happiest day in her life was the day she dropped her religion altogether. It is these immature ideas of God, and not the mature religious sentiment that is responsible for these obsessions and character-trends.

*Guilt Does Not Demand Punishment*

No analysis of the sense of sin or responsibility involves a necessary demand for punishment. A man may feel he deserves punishment, but that is a different thing from a demand for punishment. Responsibility cannot be defined in terms of 'liability to punishment' guilt may merit punishment but does not demand it. It is not punishment that necessarily follows sin, but the loss of the loved object, estrangement from our true relationship to God. Tillich gathers up the position in a sentence: 'It is not the disobedience to a law which makes an act sinful but the fact that it is the experience of man's estrangement from God, from men and from himself.'[1] It is not a judicial system which is violated when we sin but the nature of love.

## Guilt is Objective

When all allowances are made, however, for neurotic guilt, objective guilt remains undeniable. Whatever else religious guilt involves it is a blameworthy disturbance of man's relation to God. The essential moments in the experience of religious guilt are the sense of alienation from God, estrangement, the feeling that we are responsible and blameworthy for the disturbance of the relations with God; we feel guilty for what we are as well as for what we have done, even when the particular sins are uppermost in our minds. To seek forgiveness is not merely to ask for pardon but to seek the undisturbed relation with the loved object, in this case God. It is to seek a change in the governing principle of our personality; it is to seek freedom from our Ego-centricity and to become centred in God. 'For me to live is Christ', said St Paul. That is for the Christian the final aim. Substitute God for Christ and you have the aim of all the higher religions.

Practically all religions, Eastern as well as Western, offer a Salvation from the guilt-feelings and from that which thwarts the final aim. To be saved is to be rid of the burden of guilt; it is to be able to say: 'My beloved is mine and I am His.' The loved object is restored; in religious terms it is 'eternal life'.

## The Meaning of Salvation

Tillich has an interesting paragraph in which he contrasts the different meanings 'Salvation' has for different branches of the Church. 'The way in which the ultimate aim—eternal life—can be gained or lost decides about the more limited meaning of "salvation". Therefore, for the early Greek Church death and error were the things from which one needed and wanted to be saved. In the Roman Catholic Church salvation

[1] *Systematic Theology*, vol. 2, p. 53.

is from guilt and its consequences in this and the next life (in purgatory and hell). In classical Protestantism salvation is from the law, its anxiety-producing and its condemning power. In pietism and revivalism salvation is the conquest of the godless state through conversion and transformation for those who are converted. In ascetic and liberal Protestantism salvation is the conquest of special sins and progress towards moral perfection. The question of life and death in the ultimate sense has not disappeared in the latter groups (except in some forms of so-called theological humanism), but it has been pushed into the background.'[1]

Tillich takes 'salvation' to be derived from 'salvus', healing. 'In this sense, healing means reuniting that which is estranged, giving a centre to what is split between man and God, man and his world, man and himself.'[2]

Salvation, then, is the removal of everything that causes the split between man and God; especially the guilt which has caused the estrangement and alienation and within which, and indeed at its very core, there is the longing for the desired object, God. The alienation we experience is projected upon God until we become almost obsessed with the idea that He has separated Himself from us. Hence the cry of the Psalmist: 'Restore unto me the joy of Thy salvation.' He saw his sin as separating God from him. Guilt has always a positive awareness of God.

Implicit in all anxiety there is an anxiety *about* something; but also anxiety *for* something. 'Against Thee, Thee only have I sinned and done this evil', there is the anxiety *about* something; ' . . . Cast me not away from Thy presence . . . hide Thy face from my sins. . . . Purge me with hyssop and I shall be clean. . . . Create in me a clean heart, O God, and renew a right spirit within me. . . . Restore to me the joy of Thy salvation.' There you have the anxiety *for* something—the desire for the loved object.

## Guilt as Longing for the Lost Loved Object

It is this aspect of guilt-feelings—the desire for the loved

[1] *Systematic Theology*, pp. 191 f.          [2] Ibid. p. 192.

object—which the Barthians suspect of undermining the
doctrine 'All is of grace'; to them it seems to take sin too
lightly. Rather it is they who take the misery, the feeling of
unworthiness, the sense of alienation as the vital characteristics of guilt-feelings. Actually the conviction of sin is on
the surface in comparison with this deeper longing for the
God from whom our sin has separated us. The sinner himself,
under conviction is as I have said apt to project his sense of
separation upon God. Neurotic guilt does this overwhelmingly, indeed to the exclusion altogether of the longing for
the loved object. The natural desire for God, without which
there could be no religious anxiety at all, gets pushed out.
So strong is the projection of their own separation from God
in some that they come to believe that they have committed
the unforgivable sin.

The tragedy of guilt is not the intense guilt-feelings but
the lack of anxiety or guilt-feelings. That is the tragedy of
Camus's *Outsider*. It is only natural that we tend to fix our
attention on the despair, the intense misery, etc., of guilt-
feelings. When we look deeper we discover that guilt-feelings
are religiously healthy. When there are none we have Kierkegaard's *Sickness Unto Death*. To Kierkegaard religious
anxiety expresses the dynamic dissatisfaction with sin, and
is the mark of our longing for God. It is the sign to Kierkegaard that God's Spirit is still striving with us. It is the
sign that we are alienated from Him but not that we are
wholly separated from Him.

Here I would agree with Dr Torrance's implication that
the anxiety and guilt-feelings connected with mental illness
in our day, and which preoccupies the pages of our novelists
and poets, is due to the fact that guilt is divorced from the
real source, namely, alienation from God, the object of
anxious longing. Psychologically the anxiety can be expressed
in terms of the thwarting of what Hadfield calls 'The urge
to completeness', or as it has otherwise been termed 'The
prospective aim of personality'. In theological terms, it is the
thwarting of The Image of God, the religious *telos* of personality. The mentally ill person experiences this lack of

completeness, the blocking of his personality, he feels that the very aim of personality is lost: 'I have nothing to live for' he repeats endlessly. He has divorced his sense of the urge to completeness and its consequent anxiety from religion and Redemption. In Torrance's language: neither the patient nor the psychiatrist has dealt 'with man's deepest root of the problem which is sin and guilt before God'. The guilt is displaced, and becomes either psychosomatic disease or mental illness.

## Psychiatry has no Technique Whereby it could Dissipate Real Guilt

It is here we see the gulf between the psychiatrist's treatment of guilt and that of religion. The psychiatrist has no technique whereby he can deal with real guilt. To dissipate unrealistic guilt-feelings due to wrong concepts is not a difficult task. But what will he do when he finds that the displaced guilt-feelings really stem from real guilt which has become disguised? He can lay bare character-trends; show where the real defects of personality are rooted. But what will he do with the real guilt when the displaced guilt is revealed for what it is? He cannot offer forgiveness which alone can lift the burden. He cannot offer a meaning to life, nor the affection for which the patient is seeking.

## The Psychiatrist's Limitations

Jung brings out the limitations of psychiatry in an illuminating passage in *Modern Man in Search of a Soul*. 'The patient', he writes, 'is looking for something that will take possession of him and give meaning and form to the confusion of his neurotic mind.

'Is the doctor equal to this task? To begin with, he will probably hand over his patient to the clergyman or philosopher, or abandon him to that perplexity which is the special note of our day. As a doctor he is not required to have a finished outlook on life, and his professional conscience does not demand it of him. But what will he do when he sees only too clearly why his patient is ill, when he sees that it arises from his having no love, but only sexuality; no faith because he is afraid to grope in the dark; no hope, because he is disillusioned by the world and life; and no understanding because he has failed to read the meaning of his own existence?

'There are many well educated patients who flatly refuse to consult the clergyman. With the philosopher they will have even less to do, for the history of philosophy leaves them cold, and intellectual problems seem to them barren. And where are the great and wise men who do not merely talk about the meaning of life and the world, but really possess it? Human thought cannot conceive any system of final truth that could give the patient what he needs in order to live: that is, faith, hope, love and insight.

'These four highest achievements of human effort are so many gifts of grace which are neither to be taught nor learned, neither given nor taken, neither withheld nor earned, since they come through experience which is something *given* and therefore beyond the reach of human caprice. . . . "It is in reality the priest or clergyman rather than the doctor who should be most concerned with the problem of spiritual suffering."' [1]

Gordon Allport in his *The Individual and his Religion* sees psychotherapy as the ally of religion, yet he like Jung is not unmindful of its limitations; and remarks that in the United States with the best hospital facilities mental suffering has increased: 'statistically viewed, the success of modern psychotherapy has been up till now not merely negligible but negative.' So far it has failed to give the patient what he needs to satisfy the prospective aim of personality or the dissipation of guilt. 'Psychotherapy,' he writes, 'knows the healing power of love but finds itself unable to do much about it . . . the psychotherapist finds himself unable to supply the love the patient needs, or to receive the love the patient wants to give. The normal stage of "transference" in the course of treatment betrays this need, but it is a temporary step. Transference must be broken.' [2] The psychotherapist accepts the patient as he is; he is not shocked by his revelations, or

[1] pp. 260 ff.
[2] Allport, pp. 90 f.

his findings of lust, aggressiveness, hypocrisy, fear or perversions, etc., but he cannot be a substitute for God from Whom these things have alienated his patient. The one cure for the burden of guilt is forgiveness and that he cannot give. He may attempt to belittle the guilt, to ignore the moral and spiritual problem, but he finds his patient does not get better. Religion wins its way (and preachers should remember this) not by the revelation of the sinfulness of man, or his total depravity; what gives religion its authority and power is its offer of forgiveness. As one New Testament scholar said to me: 'The New Testament is a thesis on forgiveness.'

I am aware that it is possible to accuse me of having dealt more with subjective guilt than objective guilt, as the theologian sees it. Nevertheless I can accept Dr Torrance's account of objective guilt. Just as Law sees guilt as the violation of the law of the land, and the ethical philosopher sees it as the betrayal of duty or a violation of the moral law, so the theologian sees it as sin against God, His love and His holiness. Religious guilt cannot be explained in purely psychological terms any more than psychology can be a basis for ethics. Sin, with a capital letter, is, as Brunner so often reiterates, the violation of the first commandment: 'I am the Lord Thy God, thou shalt have no other Gods beside me.' Personally I prefer Christ's interpretation of this commandment: 'Hear, O Israel, the Lord our God is one Lord: And thou shalt love the Lord with all thy heart, and with all thy soul, and with all thy mind and with all thy strength: this is the first commandment.'

Brunner, clinging to the Old Testament rendering is compelled to take a judicial view of the relationship between man and God. To take one quotation:

'The more real guilt is in us the more real is the gulf between us and God, the more real the wrath of God, and the inviolable character of the law of penalty; the more real also the obstacle between God and man becomes, the more necessary becomes the transaction by means of which the obstacle, in all its reality is removed. The more serious our view of guilt, the more clearly we perceive the necessity for an objective—

and not merely a subjective—Atonement. To deny this neces-sity means the *nondum consideravisse pondus peccati.*'[1]

I can accept every word of this if we mean by 'obstacle' not something judicial, but a tension within the love of God; and if we mean by 'Wrath' something different from resentment characteristic of human anger. The 'obstacle' cannot be some-thing external to both God and man. The Law as Brunner seems to imply is something man has to obey and God has to see that it is obeyed or exact penalty if broken.

### The Meaning of 'Wrath of God'

Both these theological concepts have proved difficult of interpretation. Various theories have been expounded to get round the idea of attributing one of the 'deadly' sins to God. Father Danielou rightly notes that 'Any modern child may learn from his catechism that anger is a sin: so it is no wonder if he is shocked to hear of it in God'. He adds: 'There is hardly anything in the terminology of religion that gives more offence to the pious (or prudish) ears of the modern world than this expression, the wrath of God. It was already something of an embarrassment to the Alexandrian Jews, who attempted, in discussion with the Greek philosophers, to water it down. In our own day, Simone Weil, for example, finds it simply intolerable: for she, like Marcion of old, con-trasts the New Testament God of love with an Old Testament God of Wrath. Unfortunately for the position, there is love in the Old Testament, and there is wrath in the New—as Tertullian pointed out long ago. We have to reckon, whether we like it or not, with wrath as one of the divine attributes: and, what is more, for all its anthropomorphic appearance, this particular word may carry a stronger charge of mystical significance than any other, and afford the deepest insight into the meaning of the divine transcendence.'

He quotes Péguy to the effect that 'Wrath is the emotional response of a sound personality to anything vile, low and mean'. His own conclusion is 'that the innermost kernel of this idea of the wrath of God would be simply a mark of the

---

[1] *The Mediator*, p. 451.

intensity of his being, and the irresistible force with which his power may be manifested in creation, when he is pleased to give a violent reminder of his existence to a world steadfastly turns away from him.

'Wrath, so understood, is purged of every connotation of pettiness, meaning simply that intensity of existence which nothing whatever can withstand. It is a precious conception.'[1]

I doubt if the concept can be dissolved into the meaning of 'a person's own vitality and self-expression' with 'no reference to an object'. His illustrations are largely taken from God's 'Irresistible progress through nature and history' as seen in the third chapter of Habakkuk. He acknowledges that 'anger' and 'love' when brought together, 'as simultaneously indicating two equally essential aspects of the Godhead . . . are indeed irreconcilable at the level of human understanding: 'If God is good, how can he be so stern and angry?' 'The theological answer is that the two qualities are really one and the same in God himself, though we can only conceive them as distinct.'[2]

A very naturalistic interpretation of this difficult concept is given by Professor Daniel Williams: 'Wrath', he writes, 'means that life has within it certain ineluctible structural principles which can be defied only at the risk of losing the good life itself. When these are defied there is set in motion whether in the individual life or in the social order, a chain of consequences which may take the form of vast destruction and misery; or which may work silently in the individual soul in the loss of the meaning of life, and the fading of the glory—but it happens.'[3] This is just the old idea of penalty for sin being automatic and impersonal and I doubt if anything in the New Testament could be found as a ground for this position. It is no good shirking the fact that 'wrath' is a personal attribute. One is compelled to ask Professor Williams: 'What are these principles?' St Paul made the wrath of God personal because for him the *personal reality* of God stands behind everything.

[1] *The Lord of History*, pp. 154 f.
[2] Ibid, p. 163.
[3] *God's Grace And Men's Hope*, p. 53.

Professor C. H. Dodd attempted to equate 'wrath of God' with the impersonal law of retribution; but he failed to convince New Testament scholars.

Psychologists make short work of the difficulty. To them the wrath of God is simply the projection of the ruthlessness of the Super-ego. The demands of the Super-ego for punishment are projected upon God, and the wrath of the earthly father, introjected into the content of the Super-ego is transferred to God.

I do not doubt that we do project upon God many of our ideas and feelings; in many ways we make Him in our own image. Nevertheless, I doubt very much whether it is possible to reduce the idea of the wrath of God to subjective feelings. That would be an extreme example of 'psychologism'. We do meet in nature those 'ineluctible structural principles' which we defy at our peril. Wrath and mercy seem to intermingle in man, nature and history. Holy love surely cannot but react to the violations of love without wrath. Our fault, it seems to me, is to equate human wrath, which has always an element of vengeance and vindictiveness in it, with the wrath of God. God cannot but feel revulsion at sin: He would repel the sinner. The old tag that God loves the sinner but hates his sin is a contradiction in terms. There is no sin without a sinner; it is the sinner that is blameworthy not the sin. But we can be 'angry and sin not', that is to say, there is no vindictiveness in our anger. Our anger with a loved one has always an element of mercy in it. In our next chapter we shall see that man's sin sets up a tension within God's love for man. Indeed this is the 'obstacle' which has to be removed before forgiveness is possible. It is this overcoming of the tension within Himself which 'costs' God something and gives us the objective element in the Atonement which Brunner demands. Something happens in God as well as in man before reconciliation is possible. But there is no vindictiveness to overcome.

Religious guilt-feelings, then, or religious anxiety, cannot be explained in purely psychological terms. Religious guilt is not merely a 'sense of wronging', or an 'emotional attitude' involving emotional conflict, but a ruling principle of the personality from which stem our particular sins. That ruling principle involves the turning away from God (unbelief), resistance to His love and will (hubris); it puts the ego where God should be at the centre of one's life; that concupiscence or distorted libido which exploits others for one's own pleasure or gain. That is one side of guilt. The other is that the sense of anxiety which accompanies all guilt-feelings, is an anxiety or an anxious longing for the lost ideal or the lost loved object. Consciously or unconsciously it is a longing for God, or in the words of the *Shorter Catechism*, the desire 'to glorify God and to enjoy Him for ever'.

### SELECTED BOOKS

*Modern Theories of Sin.* W. E. Orchard, London, James Clark.

*The Individual and His Religion.* Gordon Allport, London, Constable.

*Psychology, Psychotherapy and Evangelicalism.* John G. McKenzie, London, George Allen & Unwin.

*Theory of Disease.* By Dr Guirdham, London, George Allen & Unwin.

*Neurosis and Human Growth.* Karen Horney, London, Routledge & Kegan Paul.

*The Fear of God.* Fred Berthold, Jr., New York, Harper.

*Systematic Theology.* Vol. 2. Paul Tillich, London, Nisbet.

*The Boundaries of Science.* John MacMurray, London, Faber & Faber.

# CHAPTER 6

# THE DISSIPATION OF GUILT

ONE of the main problems of psychiatry as it is of religion is the dissipation of guilt-feelings and the lifting of the burden of guilt. As we have seen psychiatry has no technique whereby it can restore the peace to a mind which is burdened with objective guilt. It cannot satisfy that longing for restored inter-personal relations. Nevertheless it has its contribution to make in spite of the Barthian anathema, and the suspicions of many theologians.

That there has been a tendency to reduce the subject matter of religion to psychological data no one will deny who has read Flügel's *Man, Morals and Society*, or Ayer's *Language, Truth and Logic*. But there is a danger of 'theologism' as well as 'psychologism'. Both are consequent on undue abstraction. As a corrective of reducing religion to psychological data credit must be given to the 'Theology of Crisis', but has it not gone too far? 'Desire to find a basis for making statements about divine revelation which will not be affected by the facts of psychological and culture conditioning (though the occurrence of such conditioning is not denied) has been carried to illegitimate lengths. Granting that the primary data of theology are not merely psychological phenomena, it is only a professionally acquired blindness to the concrete conditions and limitations of human existence, including the existence of the Church, which prompts the theologian to forget that examination of the human pole of the 'I—Thou' relationship is an integral part of his task.'[1]

I believe that there is no aspect of the 'I—Thou' relationship that needs to be explicated more than the dissipation of guilt in the forgiveness of sins. I make no apology for

[1] *Psychology and the Christian Doctrine of Man* by David E. Roberts, p. 153.

approaching the problem of forgiveness and Atonement from the 'human pole'.

## Approaches to the Problem of Forgiveness

The relation between theology and psychology is an intimate one. Psychology analyses and describes the experiences; theology formulates its doctrines in relation to the objects of those experiences. Psychology has no technique whereby it could validate or invalidate the doctrine of God, the Incarnation, the Atonement or the Resurrection; but it does accept as psychological fact that men have experiences which relate to these doctrines. 'I saw God high and lifted up' is an experience; 'I live, yet not I but Christ liveth in me' is an experience. 'There is now, therefore, no condemnation to them that are in Christ Jesus' is an experience. Everyone of these experiences involve theological dogma; the concepts on which the dogmas are built may be true or false, but the experience is nevertheless psychologically real.

The central and indeed the crucial experience of the Christian believer is that of being reconciled to God, of being at one with Him, of sins pardoned, of himself as forgiven, of being right with God. His experience of being reconciled or forgiven is immediate in exactly the same way as I have an experience of a patch of colour. I may be mistaken as to the object the patch of colour represents: but there can be no question as to the reality of the subjective experience. Even if my experience be an hallucination, it is, nevertheless, subjectively real, and must be accounted for. So with my experience of forgiveness and reconciliation: I may be wrong in referring those experiences to something that happened on the Cross; nevertheless, the experience would not be invalidated, but only the reference; the experience would still be psychologically real.

Personally I believe that the psychologist could go further than this. In every sense-perception the externality of the object is part of the *given*. The externality of the object of perception is something immediately given within the experience itself and not an inference. Analogously I might argue that the element of objectivity in my religious experience is an authentic and given part of that experience. And I do not see that anyone could confute me except on grounds that would involve the denial of the external world and all moral and aesthetic values as objective.

Be that as it may, the psychological approach to the problem of Atonement is through the analysis of forgiveness, beginning with the conviction of sin, the sense of alienation, the acceptance and realization of forgiveness and reconciliation through my repentance. The theological approach, on the other hand, is through the intellectual concepts of the nature of God, the nature of man, and the nature of sin as revealed.

Now, there is a fundamental difference between these two modes of approach to the problem of Atonement. The theological approach may involve nothing more than an intellectual insight into the relations between my concepts of God and the nature of man, and the nature of sin 'as seen by the eyes of the Father'. Intellectually I may recognize the relation between retribution and sin and yet never myself experience the conviction of sin nor the sense of alienation which sin involves. For an adequate theory of Atonement to be formulated experience and reflection must go hand in hand. Just as sensation without thought is blind, so experience without reflection is not likely to yield the *modus operandi* of Atonement. On the other hand, thought must have experience on which to reflect; otherwise it is divorced from reality. If religion is an 'experience of reality' a sharing of the life of God, then it would seem that theology cannot afford to neglect the psychological analysis of religious experience.

Here, then, is the psychologist's justification for intruding into the realm of theology. It is as a necessary co-labourer with the theologian that he attempts to elucidate the experience of the forgiveness of sins. To do his share of the task well he should have no presuppositions; he should have no preferences for this theory or that. Naturally, when he has finished his task he will have preference for the theory which takes account of the psychological data.

## Psychological Questions Raised by Forgiveness

What, then, is the experience of forgiveness and the dissipation of guilt-feelings? What does it mean to be reconciled to God? In the analysis of the experience does the psychologist find any hint as to why forgiveness is always linked in Christian experience with the Cross? Any hint as to why God is able to forgive sin? What is it that sin violates? What is the 'obstacle' Brunner says must be removed before reconciliation can take place?

These are formidable questions; they should not, however, be beyond the psychologist's competence to answer.

We have already seen that Sins are symptoms, or better still, expressions of a principle that characterizes 'sinful' nature. That principle is Ego-centricity.

Hence it follows that it is the sinner who has to be forgiven more than the sins. The late Professor H. R. Mackintosh is on good psychological ground when he writes: 'The psychological fact that in repenting the best Christians ask pardon, not only for what they have done, but even more for what they are, signifies the truth that "sin" is predictable, strictly and in the ultimate sense, of the *self* rather than isolated acts. *We* are sinful.'[1]

Such a 'fact' shows us at once where we must look for the essence of the effects of sin. Sin disturbs the spiritual relations existing between personalities—the 'I—Thou' relationship. A gulf is created from both sides. It is not simply that by his sin an individual alienates himself from the one wronged, but the wronged becomes alienated from him. Hence the real problem of the Atonement is not how the sinner can be made to repent—the aspect on which moral theories lay stress—but how the wronged person can overcome the inevitable tendency to withdraw himself from the wrong-doer. In other words, something must happen in the wronged person if forgiveness is to be real. Forgiveness involves something happening in both the wronged and the wrong-doer, it is never one-way traffic.

[1] *The Forgiveness of Sins*, p. 62.

## Psychological Conditions of Forgiveness

That brings us to the psychological conditions of forgiveness. And from what has been said the inference follows that only personal wrongs can be forgiven because it is only against persons we can sin. Sin operates within interpersonal relations. When we speak of a person sinning against law we are using a figure of speech. The law, in so far as it corresponds to the moral law, is the expression of the Will of God, or ultimately, as the moral philosopher would say, the ultimate nature of things, which can be nothing but God. The law is not something standing over against God and the sinner which the latter must obey, and which God must see fulfilled. Even when we break the laws of society, it is society-persons we wrong. Psychologically, forgiveness cannot be a juridical or forensic term. The law never forgives. It may remit a penalty, but the conviction is recorded.

The way is now clear for a consideration of the psychological conditions of forgiveness. These conditions are not one-sided. We have seen that both sinner and sinned against are alienated. It is difficult to see how it could be otherwise in sin against God. Something must happen in God as well as in the sinner before forgiveness becomes a reality; and the crux of the problem of Atonement is: what does happen in God? And the further question: how does it happen?

It is here, I think, that the theologian and the psychologist tend to take different paths. Apart from those who hold moral theories of the Atonement the theologian almost invariably brings in a juridical element. The late Professors H. R. Mackintosh and Denney are quite emphatic on this point and they lay great emphasis on the inevitability of God's hostile reaction to Sin and to the necessity of retribution. They do not seem to be able to dissociate retribution from a juridical process. The former writes:

'The point is that the Divine character is such that whenever it encounters moral evil in saint or sinner it cannot but react against it with repelling and retributive force. Love that is worthy to be called love, confronts the evil thing with inevitable and intrinsic purity. If God did not chastise sin in the very act of forgiveness, and in the persons forgiven as a sequel to forgiving them, He would not be more loving than He is; He would cease to be God.'[1]

Dr Denney found that

'From a very early time—perhaps from the time of St Paul—the sense that reconciliation was a great achievement involving effort or tension of some kind on the part of God, has played a considerable part in theologizing on this subject. In forgiving sins, it might be said, God takes sides against Himself; He has a right to exact something from us, and for our sakes forgoes that right. His justice impels Him in one direction and His mercy in another and in the very act of pardoning men and reconciling them to Himself He must reconcile these divergent attributes.'[2]

Dr Denney freely admits that this conflict between the attributes of justice and mercy is not part of the experience of forgiveness; the idea, he thought was speculative not experiential.

From the psychological point of view there can be no question of the fact that tension has to be overcome on the part of God. The tension, however, is not between attributes of justice and mercy, nor between a natural retributive force that must exact retribution and the love that would forgive; the tension is within the love-sentiment itself. Holy love, which by its very nature must be repelled by sin is at the same moment under inevitable compulsion to 'draw us sinners in'. Love cannot but be hurt when the loved one has outraged the love; nor can love desire anything but the restoration of the sinner.

In other words, my contention is that any analysis of forgiveness will show that it is never automatic; it is never spontaneous in the sense that there is no tension to be overcome within the sentiment outraged. That tension must be expressed, and it must be overcome from within the

[1] *The Christian Experience of Forgiveness*. pp. 54 f.
[2] *The Christian Doctrine of Reconciliation*, pp. 21 f.

personality; and nothing done to 'appease' or 'propitiate' could induce forgiveness. True forgiveness is never induced from without; it must come from within.

Hence it seems to me that the psychological analysis of forgiveness gives grounds for the intuition of the Church from the very beginning that the Atonement involves an objective element, that is to say, it involves something happening in God before forgiveness could have been possible. Overlooking a fault or wrong-doing is not forgiveness; 'forgetting' about it, is not forgiveness. True forgiveness is only possible when the wronged person experiences the hurt or wound to his love sentiment, overcomes the inevitable sense of alienation created between him and the wrong-doer, and identifies himself with the wrong-doer as though the sin were his own. Forgiveness is truly object-centred; it is motivated by the wrong-doer's need. One does not forgive merely from pity for the wrong-doer, nor because one cannot bear to be alienated from another. It is a truly spiritual act, involving effort and must come entirely from within the one who forgives; it is a matter of grace.

From the psychological point of view, then, forgiveness involves what Bushnell, in his amended theory of Atonement outlined in *Forgiveness and Law,* termed 'cost' on the part of God. Brunner emphasizes the same idea in his *Mediator*: 'The more clearly we see that fellowship with God is not something which can be taken for granted, the more we see that it is "costly". And the "cost" is not paid by man. For how can sinful man himself undertake to bear the "cost" of restoring the conditions of fellowship? Thus this restoration of communion "costs" God something; even on the part of God it is not taken for granted; even in Him it can only be achieved with "labour"—as a particular event. The heavier the burden of guilt the heavier the "cost", as Luther puts it; that is, forgiveness is the precise opposite of something which is so natural that it costs no effort. The knowledge of the necessity for an objective atonement keeps pace with the progress of man in laying bare his soul to reality.'[1]

[1] *The Mediator*, pp. 453 f.

Practically every type of theology allows that God cannot be indifferent to sin; His forgiveness cannot be automatic on the repentance of the sinner. Man's repentance is the condition of forgiveness; it does not induce forgiveness; it is the condition of his acceptance of forgiveness. God suffers for man's sin; His love is wounded and outraged by it; He is alienated from the sinner; He is repelled by the sin; the spiritual relation between man and God is disturbed.

The whole problem from the psychological point of view is: How can God overcome His revulsion to man's sin? How can He express this revulsion and the suffering it causes Him? How can He bridge the gulf, overcome the inner 'obstacle' which separates Him from the sinner? That is the problem from God's side. On man's side, the problem may be formulated thus: What induces repentance? Can anything but a perfect repentance receive forgiveness and make reconciliation possible? How can we explain the age-long feeling that expiation of sin is necessary?

## The Psychological Conditions of Forgiveness from Man's Side

Before I link up the Cross with forgiveness let me analyse the psychological conditions of forgiveness. It has been usual in the theory of the Atonement to insist on the necessity of a sense of sin as a prerequisite of repentance. If what is meant is that man 'comes to himself' and sees like the prodigal how his sin has separated him from his father's house, that he must feel his sin as *Mea Culpa,* and as proceeding from a sinful nature no objection can be taken by the psychologist. Indeed psychoanalysis has for its task to lay bare the conflicts within the patient's own personality from which arise his symptoms. The sense of guilt as every practising psychotherapist knows is often a moment in the downward thrust of repression, and can lead to neurosis instead of repentance. It can generate fear instead of contrition and *metanoia.* In a true conviction of sin, or an objective sense of guilt, there is certainly the anxious longing for the loved object, and perhaps the fear of losing the loved object, in this case God;

but I doubt if there is the fear of punishment. Bitter shame and remorse, a true realization of the sinfulness of our nature and of our sins; and unqualified acceptance of our responsibility, and the consciousness of our alienation from God are all inevitable elements in a true repentance leading to *metanoia*. Without the *metanoia* there is no deep reconciliation to God. It is very probable that in all realization of guilt there is a subconscious struggle to repress the guilt, and the personality-disturbing emotions; and in the neurotic and psychotic this tendency to repress the conflict and emotions into the unconscious is more or less successful; so that instead of a penitence leading to *metanoia* we get a repression of the offending tendencies. In such a case the offending tendencies are left unmodified and no true relation to God can be established; indeed God seems more alienated than ever. In a true repentance the consciousness of outraging God's love is far more prominent than any concern of the sinner with his own fate. He may feel he is 'hell-deserving', but his anxiety is for restored relations with God as we saw in the 51st Psalm. With the *metanoia* there is the change from Ego-centricity to God-centricity; the restored spiritual relations become a conscious factor in his life and the 'joy and peace in believing' are real and lasting. Just because it is the personality, or the soul, as the preacher would say, that is changed the spiritual relations are not disturbed even when he falls into sin, simply because the *soul does not consent*.

### The Meaning of the Cross

The question now arises: How is the sinner's realization of sin and his repentance elicited? It is here that the doctrine of the Cross for the Christian theologian becomes central. Forsyth speaks of the 'Cruciality of the Cross'.

All schools of theological thought have seen the Cross as central to any theory of forgiveness. The various theories of the Atonement depend on what is believed to have happened there. It may be true that the life and teaching of Jesus have inspired the good life more than the death, as Rashdall argues; but it is at the Cross that Christian believers found their guilt-feelings dissipated, their sins pardoned and the burden lifted; there they felt reconciled to God. There can be no question by even the most sceptical of psychologists, that for generations the power of forgiveness has flowed from that Cross. There is, as the late Professor Burkitt put it to the Modernists of the Anglican Church, something inevitable about the Cross; it is linked with that grace that covers our sin. No psychologist can ignore what is linked with the deepest experiences of Christians.

Can the psychologist be of help as to what must have happened on the Cross from his knowledge of all kinds of guilt, the conditions of forgiveness and reconciliation? Can he explain why all theories of the Atonement have their triumphs in giving men the assurance of forgiveness and salvation? I think he can.

Let us summarize what happens in the process we call forgiveness. First, there must be the recognition by both sinner and sinned-against of the sin that alienates them one from the other. That alienation is a positive experience. It is felt by the sinner as an inevitable separation from the one sinned against. It is felt by God as an inevitable revulsion, even the revulsion of the wrong-doer. If that experience did not alienate God it would be difficult to see what forgiveness could mean. Spiritual relations are disturbed on both sides; they must be healed from both sides. The subjective theories of the Abelardian type admit the alienation on man's side, and their problem is: how can man become forgiveable? How can repentance be elicited? The objective theories see the alienation from God's side and their problem is: What can ward off the repelling force of God's anger? How can retribution be made?

It would seem that the psychological analysis of forgiveness enables us to synthesize the two views; it preserves the objective element and makes it creative of the subjective experience of repentance. Something happens in God and something happens in man. It can give us a theory of the Atonement that conserves both elements. On the other hand, the psychological analysis of forgiveness cannot give us a theory by itself. No theory of the Atonement can be framed without theological presuppositions. For example, it is not possible to give a theory of the Atonement divorced from a doctrine of the Incarnation. However immediate the experience of forgiveness and reconciliation is, and it is immediate, no theory of how forgiveness is possible is given in the experience itself. Our beliefs about God, the nature of sin, and the nature of man undoubtedly colour the experience itself as well as determine the acceptable theory. Every theory of the Atonement is an intellectual construct. There is no revelation of a theory of the Atonement; the revelation is of forgiveness. If we may differentiate between 'dogma' and 'doctrine' then we can say that there is the revelation of the dogma of forgiveness, but no revelation of the doctrine as to how this is possible. Doctrine arises in the inevitable attempt of the mind to find an explanation of its experiences. Experience is thus created and creative. The experience is the response of the soul of the sinner to the Revelation of forgiveness; that Revelation is made through the Cross. But the experience is also creative and is the source of the doctrine.

What I think can be inferred from the psychological analysis of forgiveness is that the Cross reveals in time and through the death of Christ how God overcomes the conflict within His own love-sentiment for man. That is the one 'obstacle' that has to be removed. The Cross reveals that God suffers for man's sin and that unless He could suffer and did suffer He could not forgive. On that Cross He reveals the 'cost' in suffering He had to endure. In human forgiveness it is the estrangement of the loved one that is most deeply felt; the wronged one feels the alienation of the wrong-doer along with his own. In psychological terms he identifies himself with the wrong-doer, and suffers as though the sin were his own. Psychologically this is 'vicarious sacrifice'; it is a suffering *not instead of the sinner*; it is a suffering *with* the sinner without which he could not forgive. It is the alienation of the wrong-doer he feels as though it were his own, even when the wrong-doer is hardened and experiences no alienation. Is that not the central thought of the story of the Prodigal?

Did not the father feel the separation of his son and the cause of it long before the lad came to himself? Had he like the elder brother felt that the son had brought shame to his house and to himself he could not have forgiven. He experienced all that the son was missing, the disturbed relations between them which the son never felt until he came to himself. He felt the 'lostness' of his son, as though he himself were lost.

Is this not what we see on the Cross? We are not beholding *a sacrifice to God*, but *the sacrifice of God*. 'The death of Christ', said F. W. Robertson long ago, 'was the sacrifice of God.' The Cross is the revelation in time of God overcoming the tension within His own being caused by sin and at the same time identifying Himself with the sinner, experiencing the alienation of the sinner from Himself. No one truly forgives who is incapable of experiencing something of the sinner's self-alienation from the one sinned against. Take a homely but familiar illustration. Here is a child who has done something wrong: grant that he is intelligent enough to see not simply that his mother is 'cross' but that she is suffering because he *could* have done it. The mother at first cannot respond to the child's 'I am sorry' without an effort, without tension to be overcome. The child senses the alienation and suffering he has caused. He fears the withdrawal of her love. Then the mother hears the sobbing coming from the room to which he has been sent; she in turn senses the child's sense of alienation, and her heart breaks in an agony of love and she clasps the child to her breast—which is forgiveness; and which bridges the gulf the child's 'naughtiness' had created between them. The experience of the mother's alienation from the child, and the suffering of the child when he senses the alienation are the two moments in the experience of repentance and forgiveness; and these two moments in the one experience lead to *metanoia*. So the mother's withdrawal from the child; then the sensing of the child's feeling of alienation and fear of losing her love, are the two moments in the experience giving forgiveness. The two are reconciled, the relations are restored as though they had never been broken.

No illustration can adequately represent what takes place in God in the experience we know as forgiveness. It is His Holy Love which is outraged rather than His Holy Will. Forgiveness is not a judicial or forensic term. When we violate His Holy Will in the physical world His overruling Providence may transform the penalty into a spiritual blessing, but it cannot remit it. The Prodigal had to eat the husks; his wasted substance could not be restored, and the memory of that experience would always bring a sorrow, nevertheless modified by the knowledge of his now perfect relations with his father. Sin may have effects outside the sphere of personal relationships, and these effects must work themselves out. It is within the sphere of personal relationships that Atonement takes place; it is in relation to God's Holy love that forgiveness is assured. God takes the burden of healing upon Himself in Christ. *There was no other good enough to pay the price of sin*; that price was paid *by God not to God*. Nothing the sinner can do for himself could bring forgiveness; forgiveness can never be merited. Forgiveness is God's act; repentance conditions the sinner's capacity to receive it.

Thus I believe we preserve both the subjective elements and the objective elements in the Atonement. The moral theories see the Cross as a manifestation of God's love, and so it is; but it is also the manifestation of the 'cost' to God in suffering before sin could be forgiven. 'God was in Christ reconciling the world to Himself.' 'God commendeth His love towards us in that while we were yet sinners Christ died for us.' He felt the alienation before we felt ours. What is the dereliction cry, but God in Christ experiencing the utmost sense of alienation that man did not and maybe cannot experience?

The very fact that Christian thinkers have always felt that a theory of the Atonement was necessary witnesses to the fact that man has always intuited that something must happen in God as well as in man before forgiveness could be a reality.

I know I am outside the realm of psychology when I say that as both God and man, Christ experienced the outraged love of God, and yet at the same time what man must feel about sin in a true repentance. He could not have experienced the sense of sin, the personal shame and sorrow which repentance involves, nor could He have experienced a personal confession of sin. Vicarious repentance and vicarious confession cannot mean that He repented or confessed instead of man, and that God accepted His repentance and confession in lieu of man's perfect repentance and confession. Nevertheless, there is a sense in which Christ must have felt what man ought to have experienced. He saw sin in all its violence; He felt how it alienated from God; He experienced His own condemnation of it. In any other sense vicarious repentance and confession would seem to be psychologically impossible. I cannot repent for another although I can experience in virtue of the process of identification all the pangs of Hell that a loved one of mine ought to feel and must feel before forgiveness can be a reality. My suffering may induce repentance in that loved one; through the sensing of my sorrow for him he may intuit and thus elicit what he ought to feel. It is in this sense, I think, that we may find some truth in the theories of McLeod Campbell and Moberley.

## Does God Suffer?

Theologians will be quick to infer that the basis of a psychological theory of Atonement I have outlined involves the concept of God's passibility. I have said that 'God in Christ' suffers, and from the psychological point of view it is difficult to conceive of a love that is incapable of suffering for the loved one. If we say that God is love, that he forgives sin, we are really saying that He suffers. A love that is impassible is inconceivable by man, and contrary to all human experience. It is only as the heart is kept open to receive the wrong-doer that forgiveness is possible, and it can only be kept open through suffering. The Holier the love the deeper it is and the more capable of suffering. It would seem, then, that instead of God being impassible He is the most passible of beings. And it is just because He is pure Holy love that He can forgive absolutely.

Some theologians contend that a perfect penitence alone can guarantee an absolute forgiveness; and thus are compelled to posit a perfect penitence on the part of Christ for man which each one of us appropriates. Apart from such a demand for a perfect penitence as the condition of Atonement, this would make forgiveness a 'transaction' (a horrible word). Penitence is the condition of our receiving forgiveness, not the cause of forgiveness. Forgiveness, human or divine, can never be merited; it is all of grace. When we are forgiven we are absolutely forgiven, just as when we are guilty we are hopelessly guilty.

A word may be added here as to what is involved psychologically, in repentance. Repentance has two moments—*penitenia* and *metanoia*. Sorrow for sin may be sincere and yet not involve *metanoia*. We still continue to sin in spite of penitence and forgiveness. Why should this be? It is because however sincere the penitence, the *metanoia*, the change of mind, the 'amendment' as Father White calls it, is imperfect. To the degree we are penitent the soul cannot consent to sin, we are coerced, or rather give way to the solicitations of our motives. We hate the very thing we are doing. But to the degree there is *metanoia*, this change of mind towards the sinful tendencies, we cannot repeat the sin; the whole personality is changed. The danger of mass evangelism is that it stimulates fear of sin rather than creates *metanoia*.

## The Triumphs of Theories of Atonement

A final word may be said as to why all theories of the Atonement have their triumphs in eliciting the intuition that God forgives. The dogma is intuited, not the doctrine. It is not the truth of the doctrine which elicits knowledge of forgiveness nor even the repentance. Every doctrine of Atonement contains the offer of forgiveness; it is this which is intuited. The fact that the Penal theory of the Atonement still elicits the intuition that God forgives is due to the psychological fact that in many people their sense of guilt has a strong punitive element; their conscience demands punishment. The attraction of the theory lies in the fact that it offers to the punitive conscience a substitute Who has borne their punishment, and all that remains is for them to appropriate it. The Satisfaction Theory can only grip those who can believe that the merit of one can cancel the debt owed by another. The moral theories will always appeal for they offer the Loved Object as still loving them. It will always have its appeal also for those whose first movements towards God, and fellowship with Him, were not motivated by any fear of sin or deep conviction of sin, that conviction growing with their growth in grace. The vital thing is not the truth of this theory of Atonement or that but the offer of forgiveness.

## Religious Ideas in Mental Illness

Sin, guilt, Atonement, are at the very centre of the Church's teaching. Not seldom this is brought against her as tending to create the morbid states seen so often in mentally disturbed people. That religious ideas can be found in neurotic and psychotic persons no one could deny. That is because in the mentally ill person his religion often becomes a matter of life and death. Actually his struggle to maintain his religious beliefs is a struggle to cling to the one thing that to him gives meaning to his life and he is in fear of losing it. His religious ideas, however, are not causal factors in his illness, but the means of communicating his disturbed state. People talk about 'religious Mania', but as Dr Stafford Clark has pointed out 'The psychiatrist does not recognize religious mania as a separate illness but sees it as the form that mania may take in a religious person'.[1] Rightly, he points out that when a keen business man breaks down his 'whole talk is of business projects': he may be obsessed with the fear that his prosperous business is going bankrupt; he may complain that he cannot cope with its demands and shuts himself away from it. Yet we never talk about 'business mania'. Unfortunately the distortions of immature religion can be misunderstood by the psychiatrist and minister, as Dr Wayne Oates has well pointed out in his *Religious Factors in Mental Illness.*[2] This widens the gulf in communication and the possibility of co-operation

[1] *Christian Essays in Psychiatry*, p. 182.    [2] See the Preface.

between the two professions which deal with the illnesses of the soul.

To the degree the psychiatrist fails to understand the patient's religious talk he is likely to belittle the patient's religion and he will fail to realize that the patient is communicating something vital to the understanding of the man's inner conflicts. He may, as Thouless suggests, tend to turn the patient away from religion when 'The recovery of mental health may not be by the turning of the patient away from his religious ideas, but by leading him through these to a more balanced attitude in which he accepts the whole of the religious system of ideas and not only a part of it'. The religious system as a whole not only condemns sin, but balances the sin and guilt with the doctrine of forgiveness. Hence as Thouless puts it: 'In all such cases, there is a distortion of religious ideas, since in both the set of religious ideas connected with the guilt of sin is disconnected from the set of ideas connected with repentance and forgiveness.'

So if a minister fails to read the real meaning of what the one he is counselling is telling him he may accentuate the guilt and become a positive danger to the depressed, the obsessional and the melancholic.

But the same applies in the preaching of religion. Too much emphasis can be laid on the sinfulness of sin, and too little on the doctrine which balances our guilt, namely forgiveness. Probably this is why Whitehead preferred the Apostle John to the Apostle Paul.

Be that as it may, *the preaching of Atonement should have its greatest emphasis upon what was done for us on the Cross and not what sent Jesus to it.* Even the late Professor H. R. Mackintosh, whose evangelicalism no one could deny wrote: 'We are wise if we shut our eyes from "looking upon evil", and decide that it is unprofitable to meditate on our own wrong-doing.' Too much emphasis upon our sinfulness tends to make people seek to avoid sin rather than to make them aspire to holiness. The fear of committing sin is a neurotic symptom, characteristic of the individual obsessed by scruples or 'spiritual vermin' rather than the sign of a growth in grace.

## Pastoral Psychology and Pastoral Theology

The prevalence of religious ideas, religious anxiety and religious guilt in mental illness should be a challenge to the psychiatrist both to understand the religious life as well as religious beliefs. On the other hand the minister and the theologian would do well, as the late David Roberts wrote, to incorporate in their doctrine of bondage to sin the psychotherapist's description of bondage to inner conflicts; he should learn also from the psychiatrist that when someone comes with a confession of sin, the first thing to do is to accept him and not to judge him, to understand him before he condemns him. Psychiatry needs the faith, love, hope and insight of religion as to how God deals with guilt and sin. He has to recognize his limitations that when he has laid bare the real sin underlying the displaced guilt feelings he has then to deal with real guilt. It is then he realizes the limitations of his technique. Fortunate for him if he can see his 'task within the framework of a Christian view of man and God';[1] more fortunate still, if as a Christian, he can speak of forgiveness out of his own experience. It is then that psychiatry knows the therapeutic value of Atonement and its theories. I have known a therapist who knew how to give peace of mind to a patient with a punitive conscience by explaining to him the Penal theory of the Atonement. The punitive conscience demands punishment for its sins; but no self-punishment gives him peace; but the knowledge that expiation has been accomplished by God Himself on the Cross brings what no analysis of the patient could bring. The same therapist told me of a minister who recounted to him his conversion. He was in his late teens; experienced the conviction of sin in some tent meeting. For three days he was in Hell with fear. He could not believe that the debt he owed to God for his sins could be paid, and that for him there was nothing but Hell. Then the evangelist or counsellor took him to a room, placed a Bible on a desk, and said: 'That Bible represents your sins; the desk it is resting upon is you.' Then the evangelist took the Bible and placed it on another desk, and said: 'Now your

[1] *Psychotherapy and the Christian Doctrine of Man*, pp. 153 f.

sins are not resting upon you; they are resting on Christ on
the Cross. You are not bearing them any more.' 'In that
moment', said the minister, 'the weight of guilt was lifted
and I was free from the burden of guilt and could have
walked on air.' I think that it is Jung who calls this form of
treatment 'The healing fiction'. But that 'healing fiction' is
the function of all our religious symbols. Psychologically they
work, and they work because somehow they elicit the healing
intuition of the forgiveness of sins. There are a whole host of
psychiatric problems which simply cannot be dealt with outside a religious reference.

On the other hand, ministers must beware of attempting to
become amateur psychiatrists, and of falling into the fallacy
that all they have to do with those who come to their vestries
for counselling is to apply psychological concepts or methods.
There is all the difference in the world between pastoral
psychology and pastoral theology. The former can absorb the
insights psychology has given us into the conflicts of man,
and its technique can help us to get the parishioner to talk
his problem up. It is then that pastoral theology becomes
relevant, for the minister's help derives not from psychology
then, but from the application of Christian experience and
Christian doctrine. Pastoral theology is the wider discipline;
it includes pastoral psychology.[1]

## Change in the Pattern of Psychological Symptoms

I know many ministers are fascinated by psychoanalytic
technique and some of the Freudian concepts of the
underlying factors in mental illness, anxiety and depression.
Actually, however, as Rollo May has pointed out, patients do
not come with the same problems as they did in the earlier
day of psychoanalysis. At the beginning of the century
Victorian sex taboos were still operative; and there can be
no question but that a great many people suffered from sex
repression. Ignorance of sex, lack of opportunities to satisfy
it, and even fear of it burdened many souls. 'But in our day',
writes May, 'sexual taboos are much weaker; the Kinsey

[1] Cf. *Pastoral Care in A Changing World*, by Erastus Evans.

report made that clear if anyone still doubted it. Oppor-tunities for sexual gratification can be found without too much trouble by people who do not have pronounced other problems. The sexual problems people bring today for therapy, furthermore, are rarely struggles against social prohibitions as such, but much more often deficiencies within themselves, such as lack of potency or lack of capacity to have strong feelings in responding to the sexual partner. In other words, the most common problem now is not social taboos on sexual activity or guilt about sex itself, but the fact that sex for so many people is an empty, mechanical and vacuous experience.'

'It may sound surprising when I say, on the basis of my own clinical practice as well as that of my psychological and psychiatric colleagues, that the chief problem of people in the middle decade of the twentieth century is *emptiness*. . . .

'Many people could say out of their own experience the prophetic words of T. S. Eliot,

> We are the hollow men
> We are the stuffed men
> Leaning together
> Headpiece filled with straw. Alas!
> Shape without form, shade without colour,
> Paralyzed force, gesture without motion.' [1]

If my own experience is any guide this is true for Britain. Emptiness, hollowness, meaninglessness, loneliness—these are the main problems brought to the psychotherapist today.

Jung remarks in his *Practice of Psychotherapy*, 'About one-third of my cases are not suffering from any clinically definable neurosis but from the senselessness and aimlessness of their lives. I should not object if this were called the general neurosis of the age'.[2] I might quote Viktor Frankl, and others to the same effect.

But as we saw in the previous quotation from Jung, what can the doctor do? It is not his job to show that life has meaning and sense; it is the minister's task. It is his function to deal

[1] *Man's Search For Himself*, pp. 14 f.      [2] p. 41.

with those who are morally adrift, to give a spiritual meaning to life, to bring into a world that has lost its values, the spiritual dimension of life. At the beginning of the century we could speak about a 'lost soul'; today we have a lost generation. No application of psychological principles will give a man a meaning to life, nor will it fill his emptiness, nor take away the burden of guilt he experiences in his estrangement from his true being. Religion alone can do that.

Hence the minister is wise if he realizes that actually his theology is more important than his knowledge of psychology. The more he knows of pastoral theology which includes pastoral psychology the more effective will he be in dealing with the spiritual problems of his parishioners and of the world.

### SELECTED BOOKS

*Psychotherapy and the Christian Doctrine of Man.* David E. Roberts, New York, Scribner's, Charles, Sons.
*The Image of God in Man.* David Cairns, London, S.C.M. Press.
*The Mediator.* Emil Brunner, London, Lutterworth Press.
*The Forgiveness of Sin.* H. R. Mackintosh, London, Nisbet.
*Christ and Conscience.* N. H. G. Robinson, London, Nisbet.

# CHAPTER 7

# CONCLUSIONS

THE enquiry into the meaning of guilt and its significance has been very largely made from the psychological point of view. Although the approach is far from being purely Freudian, depth-psychology concepts underlie not a little of what I have written. That is inevitable; for we cannot divorce modern psychology from the other disciplines which have, for part of their subject matter at least, human nature and human behaviour. The day is past when either law, ethics or theology could go its own way without taking into account what depth-psychology has revealed in regard to the motivations of behaviour. These disciplines cannot simply be satisfied to co-exist with modern psychology; the relationship must be one of inter-penetration. The psychoanalyst, for example, must not think he has accounted for the sense of ought or obligation when he has traced its origin to the Super-ego. The sense of responsibility cannot be explained either by the child's fear of the reproaches of the parents or teachers, or the fear of consequences. The sense of ought belongs to the nature of things. That does not mean that the moral principles we teach the child or the ethical ideals we keep in front of his growing mind are necessarily justified. Depth-psychology may be able to explain the content of the ought, but it cannot account for our being 'ethical animals'. Dogs have 'Super-egos' in so far as they obey their masters; but they have no conscience, no sense of ought. On the other hand, depth-psychology has a right to demand that the moral principles and ethical ideals taught shall be consistent with what we know of the law of the development of moral personality. We need to know what human nature is; so that we are not trying to make it what it was never meant to become. Law, ethics and theology must take account of the insights depth-psychology has brought us if their sanctions are to be really relevant to behaviour.

That means that the relation between these disciplines should be one of mutual inter-penetration. The depth-psychologist must realize that ethical theory cannot be reduced to a psychology of morals, and ethics and theology have to acknowledge that human behaviour is always within a psychological field. What psychology can do is to throw light on what we might call the natural history of morals; in other words how the moral rules and sentiments are acquired or developed.

In the treatment of the origin and development of Super-ego and conscience we see this interpenetration at work.

The sense of ought and responsibility is not born with the rise of the Super-ego. The Super-ego does not give us the 'ought'; it gives us the 'musts' and the 'must-nots' with which the child must comply, not the sense that we *ought* to obey. That comes with the awakening of the sense of responsibility. The sense of ought and responsibility belong to the nature of things; they involve that in the nature of things there is a moral order to which man can conform, indeed must conform if he is to develop the potentialities of his moral nature.

Depth-psychology in its understanding of psychological and moral conflict has revealed to us in the analysis of psychosomatic and mental illness the ways in which it is possible to try and escape from that moral order. This points to the fact that man's nature has a teleological aim; that like every living thing it has a *telos*. In theological terms the *telos* is the *Image of God* fully seen in Jesus, and to which we are to be conformed.

What we conclude from this study of the development of the conscience is that man is fundamentally an 'ethical animal', to use Waddington's term. His sense of guilt shows that he is estranged from both his ethical essence and his religious end. That ethical guilt is not to be taken as a sign of an inherently evil nature, but is a longing to realize his ethical essence and his religious end. Always anxiety (and guilt is anxiety with a special quality) is a longing for the estrangement to cease. The fact that he experiences guilt-feelings is the hall-mark of his sense of responsibility and that he has really become human.

Our study of legal guilt brought us into touch with the antagonism between psychiatry and law. As a definition of insanity or a criterion of responsibility the McNaghten Rules are thought of as being out of touch with what depth-psychology has revealed of the mental conflicts and compulsive impulses which often lead to crime. Judges and lawyers are being influenced by psychology; and there can be no doubt of the anxiety of the law to see that no innocent individual is convicted of a crime he did not commit or was not responsible for committing. The fact that the Royal Commission on Capital Punishment has accepted the Scottish concept of 'diminished responsibility' and taken account of emotional disorder in the assessment of responsibility show that however difficult it may be to find criteria by which to assess responsibility and culpability, there is a strong desire to integrate with the law an understanding of the criminal, and to fit the punishment to the criminal rather than to the crime.

The question of ethical guilt raised a whole host of difficult problems. To accept the linguistic view of ethics is impossible to anyone who takes the experiential fact of guilt seriously. Value judgments cannot be so easily dismissed as the linguistic philosophers tried to make out. Just as the appetite of hunger implies the objectivity of food by which it can be satisfied, so the irreducible experience of the sense of ought and guilt imply an objective moral order to which we should conform or from which we are estranged; they imply a system of imperatives obligatory for man. The ethical judgment of behaviour instead of being meaningless is a necessary interpretation of behaviour. For surely the analysis of the term 'stole' in the proposition 'X stole his friend's purse' is that X took what did not belong to him, and had no right to take. Moral behaviour is valuated behaviour, and involves a rational judgment, and not merely an emotional one.

The vexed question of the freedom of the will one cannot hope to have answered. There is no way by which we could prove or categorically state that 'I could have done otherwise than I did'. If I had brought the considerations of my behaviour that I can see today quite clearly then I would have acted differently. But given the situation and the factors at work it is difficult to say that I could have acted otherwise. Meeting the same situation today with what I have learned from my experience yesterday I am likely to act differently. Moral behaviour is contingent, not necessitated. Alter my motives and my behaviour will be different. Our behaviour is never causeless, it is never motiveless, and it is never absolutely predictable.

Our freedom seems to lie in our capacity to learn from experience; and in the fact of self-determination, in which the Self chooses the motives from which it will act.

The meaning of ethical guilt seems to lie in the fact that we violated the moral order, which naturally includes our relations to others; we have outraged the system of imperatives by which the moral order is bound together. And the significance of the guilt is that it marks our awareness that we are separated from our ethical essence, and yet longing to realize it.

Finally we saw that theology links guilt with Sin. The whole drama of Incarnation, Passion, Atonement and Resurrection finds its meaning in relation to lifting the burden of Sin and guilt. Man is existentially estranged from his essence, which is the Image of God, by birth; but he is also estranged through Sin. In virtue of his Ego-centricity he is a sinner. The root of all sins is Ego-centricity. His guilt-feelings are the acknowledgment of his estrangement through sin; but also the expression of his anxious longing. The image of God remains and is the only source of his capacity to respond to the religious appeal to change from his Ego-centricity to God-centricity. Sin is an outrage of God's love and makes God repel him.

Nevertheless, religion alone can offer the true dissipation of guilt-feelings. It offers the restoration of the anxiously longed for loved object. The relation between the sinner and God is not judicial but filial.

The problem of how sin can be forgiven is the problem of soteriology. In the Cross theology sees the means whereby the sinner can be forgiven, reconciled and justified. The meaning of the Cross can only be understood through an analysis of forgiveness. Here we saw that forgiveness 'costs' something. The 'cost' is paid by God, not to God, in His identification of Himself with the sinner in Christ. The Cross shows God in Christ overcoming the ambivalence which sin causes in His own love for men—one tendency repulses the sinner, the other 'draws us sinners in'. That He does by experiencing the alienation of Himself and of man which sin creates. Christ was not a sacrifice to God, but the sacrifice of God.

Repentance is the condition of forgiveness.

Thus the theological meaning of guilt is that it is the violation of God's love, some would say of His will. Its significance lies in the fact that it shows man aware of his estrangement from his religious essence; but it also shows man's longing for that which he has lost.

It is here that we see where religion and psychiatry can co-operate in dealing with man's most tragic condition—his guilt. Analytical psychology (not the push-button type that can administer electric shocks) can lay bare where the roots of man's estrangement lie; but it cannot offer forgiveness; it can lay bare where man misses the meaning of life or is unadjusted to life, but it cannot give him a meaning, nor can it give him objective conditions to which he can become adjusted. Religion alone can create the faith, hope, love and insight through which his guilt-feelings are dissipated, and the way cleared for the image of God to realize itself.

Bare bones have little attraction. For these bones to be clothed in flesh one must go to the various chapters of the book.

One general conclusion comes out of the study and that is that guilt-feelings and objective guilt must be taken seriously by any student of modern life. Mental disturbance and psychosomatic illness are on the increase; crime is on the increase. How far is all this due to a weakened sense of moral responsibility? Moral philosophers have done little to deepen our sense of responsibility. If the function of philosophy is to make us aware of the deepest problems of life, can it fulfil that function unless it leads us back to think of those old but ultimate questions God, Man, and the World and the relations between them? Linguistic philosophy is not thinking things through but an escape from thinking. Not a little mental disturbance with its allied guilt-feelings is due to repression as Freud and the depth-psychologists have taught us; but repression means an escape from the moral reality of life. On the other hand, much mental illness and guilt-feelings are due to the fact that the modern world, deprived of authoritative moral or religious principles has no guide and drifts into ways of living which violate not only the moral order but the laws of personality. We cannot violate these without suffering; and our suffering today does not take the form of a fear of Hell, but a fear of insanity and the mental hospital. Man refuses to realize that he belongs to a moral order and he suffers the consequences.

Depth-psychology has discovered for us the predicament of man. It shows him estranged from his true being; it shows why he is estranged. It lays bare the deep structures of Ego-centricity which lies behind our sins, or 'complexes'; it deals with the personality as a whole. As Tillich has pointed out: 'Depth-psychology has helped theology to re-discover the demonic structures that determine our consciousness and our decisions. . . . It means that if we believe we are free in terms of conscious decision, we can find that something has happened to us which directed these decisions before we made them. The illusion of freedom in the absolute sense in which it was used is included in this discovery. This is not determinism. Existentialism is certainly not determinism. But existentialism and especially psychoanalysis and the whole philosophy of the unconscious have rediscovered the totality of personality in which not only the conscious elements are decisive.' [1]

Nevertheless, as we have seen, although psychology can discover the unconscious elements in man which cause his

[1] *Faith and Freedom*, vol. 9, p. 9. Report of an address by Paul Tillich.

predicament and estrangement it cannot of itself get him out of his predicament, nor end his estrangement. It cannot give him meaning, nor can it give him the meaning to life he needs to relate him to the moral order.

Nor can law. It can but punish; it cannot redeem. Sin and guilt must be related to redemption from which we saw it was divorced.

We are thrown back on religion. It alone has proved the real personality transformer. It alone has proved also its power to make guilt the first step to wholeness by showing that it is an anxious longing for God from Whom we are estranged. It is religion that prevents guilt from being the first step in repression that leads to pathological illness. As Marjorie Brierley writes: 'PERSONS TO WHOM RELIGION OFFERS A WORKING SOLUTION OF THEIR LIFE PROBLEMS SELDOM APPEAR IN THE CONSULTING-ROOM'.[1]

What is religion's secret? Why is it the most effective dissipator of the guilt-feelings which ravage the soul of man today? I can summarize the answer in ideas of Tillich: God accepts me unacceptable as I am; God united me with Himself; I am united to my real essence and being; and God transforms me by His indwelling Spirit. I am not merely patched up; I am made new.

[1] p. 219.

# APPENDIX 1

# THE URGE TO PUNISH

In an excellent lecture on 'Psychoanalysis and Ethics', Professor Morris Ginsberg, speaking of the contribution that psychoanalysis can make to the understanding of behaviour, said:

'Psycho-analysis can contribute to the clarification of moral experience by ridding it of the magical elements that have gathered around it and purging it of fear and anger. An example of what I have in mind is to be found in the persistent influence of the emotional demand for retribution on the criminal law and on the philosophical theories of the ethical basis of punishment. The movement in recent psycho-analytic writings towards a "humanist" ethics is clearly in this direction. But though an ethic based on love is vastly superior to one based on obedience, it will not suffice to salve the complex problems of human relations, even in small groups, and still less in the "great society". The demands of love generate conflicts of their own. There are fissures, as Freud saw, within the libido itself. To overcome them we need more than goodwill. Neither in theory nor practice can love replace justice.'[1]

That is a point of view with which both law and theology would agree. 'Justice', said one theologian, 'is deeper and more important than truth.' 'The law must fulfil its promises' as Oliver Holmes said, 'And the law is punitive. There is the urge to punish and it seems endemic in all societies.'

There is the related problem: the individual's *need* for punishment. Father White, and there are ethical philosophers who would agree with him, thinks that this need for punishment by the individual wrong-doer is endemic in human nature.

[1] Essex Hall Lecture, 1952.

Personally I do not believe you can separate the two. What light can psychology throw upon this phenomenon of the urge to punish?

There is no doubt as Gregory Zilboorg pointed out in his *Psychology of the Criminal Act,* that 'The struggle of man against another man who violates his property or life is very old, very intense, elemental; from the psychological point of view it is the same today as it was centuries ago'.

One thing is certain: all punishment is rooted in emotional attitudes. That does not mean that society has no rational grounds for punishing the evil doer; but it does mean that the emotional attitude is primary, and not the result of rational insight. A child retaliates if another child steals his toy; and the child who steals the toy shows signs that he is aware that he should not do so. To retaliate if someone violates my property involves that I feel that I should be retaliated against should I try to do the same thing. There we seem to get at the roots of justice, and the urge to punish.

Sociologically, punishment is an element in social control. Parents use it in threatening punishment to control their children's behaviour. Psychologically, punishment cures nothing; but the fear of it can restrain both the child and the adult from repeating the offence. It is admitted that as a deterrent of the person with criminal tendencies it is ineffective; and indeed in children it has often the opposite effect from that intended. For punishment to be effective it must be accepted, there must be a realization of blameworthiness. I remember being sharply pulled up by a schoolboy with whom I had been commiserating because he had received punishment at school. The boy looked astonished and replied: 'But I did what I knew I ought not to have done and I deserved it.' Such an acceptance because arising from a sense of moral responsibility, corrects the behaviour tendencies rather than just prevents him doing it again.

It is this we rightly and reasonably wish for one who has done wrong: we want him to enter the ethical community as a responsible agent; and I think that it is the desire for such realization which gives an ethical right to punish.

Such a position is as old as St Thomas Aquinas. Although holding the accepted view of punishment as a social necessity, he yet contended that if punishment was to be effective it must be accepted by the one who endures the punishment.

Accepting, then, the position that society is justified in inflicting punishment on offenders in the interests of its own safety, can we say that that justifies the 'persistent influence of the emotional demand for retribution?' The demand made in many quarters for 'condign' punishment, punishment that will fit the crime rather than the criminal is very largely due to the emotional revulsion which cruel, violent, and bestial crimes stir in the minds of us all. This is especially noticeable in crimes against children. The revulsion of feeling is accentuated by 'exhibits' in the law courts, and naturally the prosecuting counsel, and not seldom by the Judge when he passes sentence.

Nevertheless, as Professor L. T. Hobhouse wrote, if we were 'asked whether we definitely and justifiably wish evil to the bad man . . . few will answer in the affirmative. They will ride off by declaring punishment to be a good in disguise. This is to commit themselves to the reformatory theory.'[1]

Perhaps we can get light on this difficult 'persistent influence of the emotional demand for retribution' if we look at the other side of the problem: need for punishment.

This undoubtedly is morbid. It has its roots in the threats of the Super-ego. Every 'must' or 'must not' contains a threat as we saw in an earlier chapter. When a child introjects the commands or prohibitions of parents and teachers it also introjects the threatened punishment which the disobedience to the commands involved. I have seen a child bring a slipper to be punished when it had disobeyed. I saw another bash its head against the wall when punishment was refused. Not until she punished herself did she seem satisfied. 'She was following the expiatory theory.'

This morbid need for punishment is seen at its worst in neurotic people; it takes the form of self-punishment. One woman took the Biblical injunction, 'If thine eye offend

[1] *The Elements of Social Justice*, p. 125.

pluck it out' literally and blinded herself. As we have seen it is this demand for self-punishment which gives strength to certain theories of the Atonement. I do not believe that the need for punishment is endemic in human nature. Punishment as an expiation the child learns early in life; it is 'naughty', it is punished and then accepted again. That is the psychological root of the idea that wrong-doing has to be paid for. We can see it in the experience of Arthur Koestler already mentioned. The sense of guilt has always been with him except when he was in jail awaiting death for entering Spain without leave. He had now really committed a crime and his conscience is immediately silenced because he is paying for it. Few criminals resent a fair sentence although they do not like it. But they feel, 'I was caught', and as one said the other day: 'I'll have to pay the price.' We see the same thing on a harmless scale in those people who put a coin into the missionary box if they have given expression to an expletive, or come down late for breakfast. Expiation gives relief, but it does not cure. The neurotic thinks his impulses or phantasies are sinful, and every fall demands a 'forfeit'; the forfeits become higher with every fall: I have seen an individual fall into a serious mental illness in the attempt to pay the forfeit of denying that the Holy Spirit was divine. Forfeits are not only payment for a fall but also made to prevent a fall. The person says: 'If I do that again I shall deny myself this or that pleasure' until all pleasure is barred; or 'My fall will be equal to denying the divinity of Christ.' The making of morbid bargains becomes compulsive. The victims are guilt-ridden from morning until night.

I believe this demand for retributory punishment lies in this immature Super-ego. We dissociate the deed from the person, and that inhibits sympathy, the true sense of justice, and we get the clamour for severe punishment. I have noticed again and again that it is people with a ruthless Super-ego, and who habitually punish themselves, who cry for 'condign' punishment of offenders. It is not altogether untrue that those of us with repressed criminal tendencies demand severe punishment for offenders, especially if the crime stirs excessive emotions. It is a well-known fact that parents are most severe on their children when they see in them signs of their own conscious or unconscious weaknesses.

Freud was not far from the truth when he reminded us that law does not forbid acts which man is not or rarely tempted to commit. Look how hard the British Medical Association is on doctors who exploit their patients. Where the temptation is great the law is more severe.

In us all there are evil tendencies, conscious and unconscious, to anti-social acts which are either ruthlessly controlled or repressed. We have a hackneyed witness to this in the familiar phrase: 'There go I but for the Grace of God.'

Another possible explanation of this demand for retributory punishment, is unconscious envy. What our Super-ego will not allow us to do we demand to be prohibited. We begin as Dorothy Sayers said penetratingly by asking ourselves plausibly: 'Why should I not enjoy what others are enjoying?' How often have I heard promiscuous men with a strong Super-ego say that! But it ends, says Miss Sayers, by the demand: 'Why should others enjoy what I may not?' Punish them severely is the cry of the man or woman dominated strongly by unconscious envy.

That does not mean that criminality is a disease, nor that punishment cannot be justified. Deliberate choice of evil, or refusal of the good is by no means rare. We can adopt Egocentricity as the ruling principle of our lives. Apart from that there are men and women with compulsive criminal tendencies who must be restrained. It is rather the form of the punishment than punishment itself which psychologist and penologist seek to reform. But there can be no question but we get a sort of catharsis when we read of severe punishment for crimes which we have an unconscious tendency to commit. Fortunately the Super-ego is still very strong in the most mature human beings. Ruthless, it may be, if we violate its prohibitions; but it is the saviour of many.

# APPENDIX 2

# COLLECTIVE GUILT

In the text I have treated guilt as pertaining exclusively to the individual. What about collective guilt? Can we speak of a nation as guilty? In what sense can we predicate guilt of a group such as a Trade Union, or a business concern?

In law an association or group can be indicted as a 'persona ficta', that is to say it is treated as a person, and can sue or be sued at law. It can be held responsible for the actions of its servants, as well as for the activity of its board of directors. On the other hand, one could not commit the whole body of shareholders to prison. Were a body of directors indicted for issuing a false balance sheet, or a misleading prospectus they could be charged with conspiring together to cheat the public, but it would be as individuals and not as a board, and were the charge proved, each director would be held culpable according to his degree of responsibility. It is rather unlikely that they would be held equally guilty.

There is, I believe, what is called 'Company Law'; but I have not enough knowledge of it to say on what conditions a Company can be charged at law. As far as I know only a real person can be charged in a criminal court.

The idea of collective guilt was common to primitive peoples where all things were held in common; a violation of tribal rights or customs would be looked upon as a crime against the tribe. A misdemeanour on the part of one might be thought to bring down the wrath of the Gods upon the whole tribe. We have the example in Scripture of the sin of Achan whose sin was said to be responsible for the defeat of Israel by the men of Ai (Joshua vi). He and his whole family were put to death. The collective responsibility of the whole people is the basis of Israel's relation to God. Some scholars have contended that it was Israel God loved rather than the individual Jews; and that many Psalms have for their subject the whole nation rather than the experience of an individual.

Theologians have contended that the whole human race was involved in the 'Fall of Adam'. St Paul writes to the effect that in Adam all sinned: 'By one man sin entered into the world . . . by one man's disobedience many were made sinners' (Romans v).

That no man 'liveth unto himself' is an obvious truth; we are all involved in what others do. The innocent suffer with the guilty. That, according to Tillich, is part of our destiny.

Few philosophers today would uphold the concept of a 'general will' as an entity separate from the wills of individual members of a nation. Sociologists speak of a 'social mind', a 'social conscience'. They speak of the products of the social mind, such as public opinion, social memory, etc., but as far as I know there is not one who thinks the social mind or the social conscience to be anything else than the outcome of the interaction of rationally like-minded members of the community. We tend to respond emotionally in the same way in virtue of our common ideals, common interests and common background. A speaker can rouse a whole audience to a spontaneous outburst of applause; a mob can be swayed as though it were one individual. Nevertheless, there is no fusion of minds; we remain separate individuals responsible only for our own reactions.

If there is no social mind it is difficult to see how there could be collective guilt. If there is guilt at all it pertains to the individual. To the degree the individuals participate in the acts of their rulers to that degree they are guilty. As Tillich puts it:

'The individual is not guilty of crimes performed by members of his group if he himself did not commit them. The citizens of a city are not guilty of the crimes committed in their city; but they are guilty as participants in the destiny of man as a whole, and in the destiny of their city in particular; for their acts in which freedom was united with destiny have contributed to the destiny in which they participate. They are guilty, not of committing crimes of which their group is accused but of contributing to the destiny in which these crimes were committed. In the indirect sense, even the victims of tyranny in a nation are guilty of this tyranny.' [1]

Two situations in my lifetime would seem to bear out Tillich's idea here. In August 1914 when we went to war over the violation of Belgian neutrality, the late Principal Jacks, editor of the *Hibbert Journal*, wrote to the effect that what the nation felt was not the absence of discord or criticism, but the *presence of unity*. We all felt the righteousness of our cause as though we were one man. It was a collective unity; we were following our destiny. The second occasion was the rape of Czechoslovakia. There were few citizens of Britain who did not feel that they were participators in the crime against that nation. But it was guilt felt individually as if we had participated through our government in a crime against another nation. It was guilt felt in regard to our destiny rather than anything personal we had done. In both these cases we experienced 'Collective consciousness'.

I forget who said 'You cannot indict a whole nation'. I think that is ethically true. The tendency to indict Germany as a whole with collective guilt and responsibility is, as Professor H. D. Lewis[2] has pointed out, a reversion to a primitive attitude. Collective guilt has been used to rationalize the segregation and persecution of the Jews through the centuries; it was used to justify the destruction of Lidice. There are still many who think Germany collectively guilty. Curiously enough, we do not hold the Russian people collectively responsible for the 'cold war'.

It would seem, then, that moral responsibility can only be attributed to personal actions. That would, however, include the failure to take action. We are responsible for 'doing nothing' when protest or action might have altered our destiny. Afraid of war we applauded 'Munich' and its 'scrap of paper'. The guilt came to the surface with the rape of

[1] *Systematic Theology*, vol. 2, pp. 66-68.
[2] *Morals and The New Theology*, chapter 6. See also *Morals and Revelation*, pp. 102-120.

Czechoslavakia. Collective evil comes not because evil men are stronger than good men, but because the 'good' people are apt to remain aloof and inactive from the political movements of our days. Nations get the governments they deserve has a strong element of truth; and if an evil party has gained power because of the failure of 'good' people to play a good citizen's part, they share the guilt. It is this kind of thing that gives credence to the idea that a nation can be guilty.

So far as religion is concerned it is very doubtful if anyone has felt repentant for Adam's sin. Certainly the 'conviction of sin' which leads to repentance and conversion is not related in the mind of the individual with anything that occurred in the Garden of Eden! It is our own Sin and sins for which we are responsible. If we are in bondage to sin, it is not Adam's sin to which we are in bondage, but our own Ego-centricity from which all our sins stem.

# INDEX

Allport, Gordon, 101, 148
Atkins, John, 26
Auden, W. H., 13, 127
Augustine, St, 55, 116
Ayer, A. J., 91-97, 113, 148

Barth, Karl, 18, 19, 130, 132, 133
Berdyaev, N., 26 f.
Berthold, Fred, Jr. 130, 132 f.
Bowlby, Dr, 30, 47 f., 74
Bradbrook, Miss, 13
Brain, Sir Russell, 123
Braithwaite, Professor, 112
Brierley, Marjorie, 181
Broad, Professor, 89
Brunner, Emil, 135, 149 f., 152, 157, 160
Bushnell, Horace, 160

Campbell, A. C., Professor, 112, 118, 120
Cairns, D., 174
Camus, Albert, 127, 146
Cardozo, Justice, 70
Clark, Dr Stafford, 63, 64, 80, 168
Cohen, Professor John, 61 f., 84, 123
Cowper, William, 110
Curran, Dr Desmond, 78

Danielou, Father, 150 f.
Deas, Lord, 60, 69
Denny, Professor James, 158
Dodd, Professor C. H., 152
Drever, Professor James, 105

East Sir Norman, 78
Eliot, T. S., 13, 14, 127, 173
Ewing, A. C., 88, 98

Faulkner, William, 13, 127
Flügel, Professor, 41, 48, 154
Forsyth, P. T., 18 f.
Frankl, Victor, 173

Freud, Sigmund, 17, 29, 32, 36, 38, 41, 44, 47 f., 66, 68, 105, 118, 133, 180, 186
Fromm, Erich, 43-46

Ginsberg, Professor, 17, 43, 51, 182
Greene, Graham, 13
Goodhart, A. L., 81, 84 f.
Grensted, Professor, 138
Guirdham, Dr, 77, 125

Hadfield, Dr, J. A., 81, 136, 146
Hamilton, Professor K., 13
Hare, R. M., 95, 96 f., 107
Hegel, 124
Heidegger, 19
Hobhouse, L. T., 104 f., 122 f., 184
Hocking, Professor, 136
Hodgson, Leonard, 136
Holmes, Oliver Wendell, 70, 182
Horney, Karen, 43, 47, 74
Hume, David, 90, 103
Huxley, Sir Julian, 55
Hyslop, Dr, 70

Jacks, L. P., 20
Jones, Sir Henry, 100
Jones, Professor Rufus, 52 f.
Jung, 110 f., 124, 147 f., 172 f.

Kafka, 27
Kant, 124
Keith, Lord, 59
Kierkegaard, 146
Koestler, Arthur, 26, 185

Laird, Professor John, 17, 27, 87, 89, 107, 113, 115, 117, 119 f.
Laski, H., 70
Lewin, Kurt, 35 f.
Lewis, Professor, H. D., 16, 21, 89, 91, 98, 189
Luther, Martin, 160

McDougall, William, 102 g., 114
Mackintosh, Professor H. R., 136, 157, 158, 170
MacMurray, Professor John, 74, 105, 108
McNaghten (Rules), 60, 63, 65 f., 68-70, 76, 81, 83, 123, 177
May, Rollo, 172 f.
Morgan, Lloyd, 100

Niebuhr, Richard, 133
Nunberg, Dr, 75, 109

Oates, Dr Wayne, 169
Orchard, Dr, 19, 124
Otto, Dr, 30

Paul, St, 133, 135, 137, 139, 144, 170
Peel, Sir Robert, 63
Pfister, Dr 124

Rashdall, Hastings, 49, 87 f., 89 f., 93, 162
Ray, Isaac, 60, 62, 65
Roberts, David, 154, 171
Robertson, F. W., 165
Robinson, Norman, 132 f.
Ross, Sir David, 80, 110

Sartre, Jean, 13, 134
Sayers, Dorothy, 186
Seeley, Sir John, 110

Shand, A., 51
Sherrill, Lewis J., 127, 131, 141
Slater, Dr Eliot, 72, 74, 79
Smith, P. H. Nowell, 89
Stekel, Dr, 14
Stephen, Sir James, 64
Stephen, Karin, 38 f., 47, 48 f.
Stevenson, C. L., 94
Suttie, Dr Ian, 122

Tennant, Dr 124
Thomas, Saint, 184
Thouless, Professor, 170
Tillich, Paul, 19, 130, 133 ff., 138, 143 ff., 180, 188
Torrance, Professor T., 128 f., 132, 140 f., 146 f., 149

Waddington, C. H., 17, 19, 29, 34, 55, 56, 80
Ward, Professor James, 109
Warnock, Mrs, 120
Weil, Simone, 155
White, Father, 15, 20, 23, 124, 143, 168
Whitehead, Professor, 131, 170
Williams, Professor Daniel, 151
Williams, Granville, 59, 62
Winnicott, Dr, 20, 29, 34, 41 47, 48, 49, 50, 55, 74, 111

Yellowlees, Dr H., 62, 78, 81 f.
Young and Meiburg, 126

Zilboorg, Gregory, 58, 63, 65, 183

3

# Date Due